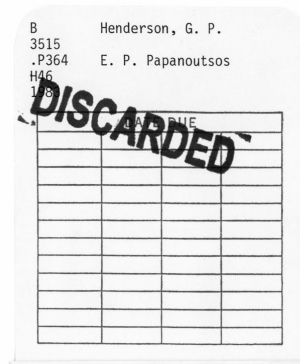

Henderson, G. P.

E. P. Papanoutsos

E. P. Papanoutsos

Twayne's World Authors Series

TWAS 678

E. P. PAPANOUTSOS
(1900–1982)

*Photograph courtesy of the Academy
of Athens Research Center for Greek
Philosophy.*

E. P. Papanoutsos

By G. P. Henderson

University of Dundee

Twayne Publishers • *Boston*

E. P. Papanoutsos

G. P. Henderson

Copyright © 1983 by G. K. Hall & Company
All Rights Reserved
Published by Twayne Publishers
A Division of G. K. Hall & Company
70 Lincoln Street
Boston, Massachusetts 02111

Book production by Marne B. Sultz
Book design by Barbara Anderson

Printed on permanent/durable acid-free
paper and bound in The United States
of America.

Library of Congress Cataloging in Publication Data

Henderson, G. P. (George Patrick)
   E. P. Papanoutsos.

   (Twayne's world authors series ; TWAS 678)
   Bibliography: p. 143
   Includes index.
   1. Papanoutsos, E. P.   I. Title.   II. Series.
B3515.P364H46   1983   199'.495   82–15902
ISBN 0–8057–6526–3

To the memory of
Hester L. D. Henderson

Contents

About the Author

George Patrick Henderson is a graduate of the Universities of St. Andrews and Oxford. After earlier academic service he became Professor of Philosophy in the University of St. Andrews (Queen's College, Dundee) in 1959 and then in the University of Dundee from 1967. The title of professor emeritus was conferred on him in 1980. He is the author of many articles and reviews in leading academic journals and was editor of *The Philosophical Quarterly* from 1962 until 1972. From 1973 until 1976 he was dean of the Faculty of Arts and Social Sciences in Dundee. Partly as a result of war service in Greece he has combined with his work in philosophy a strong interest in modern Greek language and literature; this had led to *The Revival of Greek Thought 1620–1830* (1970) and *The Ionian Academy* (in Greek translation, 1980). He has been a close literary associate of E. P. Papanoutsos for almost thirty years. In 1972 he was elected a corresponding member of the Academy of Athens, and in 1975 of the Ionian Academy. He has been a fellow of the Royal Society of Edinburgh since 1980.

Preface

For well over half a century E. P. Papanoutsos has been immersed in Greek education. He has taught and lectured, written, argued, planned, and directed—all in the cause of a modern educational system which would be liberal in its principles and constant in its regard for the individual. His struggle has been on behalf of education at all its levels and in all its forms, not only linguistic, literary, and artistic but also scientific, professional, and technological. He has seen the same basic human values as being at stake at every level and throughout these forms. Never since the beginning, however, has he made any concession to doctrinaire thinking. While motivated steadfastly by the liberal ideal he has been no mere "partisan," but has articulated that ideal for himself and thought it through to its consequences, in theory and in practice. Not surprisingly, his independence of mind has made him a controversial figure; but it is safe to suggest that his place in the history of Greek education is secure, and that it will become more secure with the passage of time.

Parallel with his educational involvement has been his involvement, as a philosophical author, with the study of human nature in its most basic aspects and developments. In the first chapter of this book an outline is given of the kind of educational program to the realization of which Papanoutsos has dedicated his public life. It is stressed, however, that there is an organic connection between that practically directed activity and the corpus of systematic philosophy which Papanoutsos has thought through, sometimes in the intervals of his public undertakings, sometimes in the very process. And it is argued that in that corpus there is a fit and proper subject to take for study on its own, as is done in this book. It is difficult to say whether Papanoutsos is better known in Greece itself as an educational reformer or as an author—so far as the two capacities can be separated. But again a safe suggestion can be offered, to the effect that his place in the history of Greek authorship is secure, and that *this* will become more secure with the passage of time.

In the second chapter of this book the author gives an account of Papanoutsos's general outlook, style, and method as a philosophical writer. The third is occupied with a critical analysis of Papanoutsos's theory of knowledge or "gnosiology," with special attention paid to the significance of that unfamiliar and awkward term. The reader should be warned that, just as the volume entitled *Gnosiology* is the most austere and difficult of Papanoutsos's works, this chapter—based largely on it—is the most austere and difficult in the present book. Chapter 4 deals with Papanoutsos's moral philosophy and Chapter 5 with his aesthetics. The reader may form the impression, as the author has done, that Papanoutsos's writings on aesthetics are among the freshest and most lively of his productions. Chapter 6 looks at Papanoutsos's views on the relationship of science, history, philosophy, and religion. In the conclusion, the author attempts to convey the essence of Papanoutsos's humanism, which he sees as running throughout Papanoutsos's literary work.

For reasons indicated in the first chapter, the author has chosen to examine Papanoutsos's philosophy topic by topic, rather than book by book. The latter course would have been tedious. Nevertheless, the discussions have been confined deliberately to the content of six works, the *Aesthetics, Ethics,* and *Gnosiology;* and what are to some extent their supplements, *Philosophy and Education, Philosophical Problems,* and *Reason and Man.* The main themes in Papanoutsos's thinking are well represented in these massive works. At that, the author has been forced, for reasons of space, to be selective in the choice of topics for discussion. His own interpretations, however, have been influenced at various points by his knowledge of Papanoutsos's thinking in general, and by a personal acquaintance with Papanoutsos extending over twenty-eight years.

A full bibliography of Papanoutsos's work would be very lengthy, but the selective one provided is sufficiently comprehensive for the purposes of this book, for two reasons: (1) that some of Papanoutsos's earlier printed work was superseded by the *Aesthetics-Ethics-Gnosiology* trilogy; (2) that many of his exceedingly numerous essays and shorter pieces, originally printed in newspapers and journals, have been collected into certain of the volumes listed. Examples of such collections are his *Passing Topics* and *Themes Topical and Otherwise.* The bibliography does include the not-very-numerous examples of Papanoutsos's work which are available in English translation. It is because his work in Greek is bound to be inaccessible to very many readers that the opportunity has been taken in this book to include a fair number of excerpts from it, all in translation by the author.

Papanoutsos writes in an elegant, flowing style of Greek which might be termed "scholarly demotic." One of his great educational preoccupations has been the defense and the cultivation of demotic, the natural language of the modern Greek people, for scholarly and scientific purposes, as well as those of imaginative literature. His own work is a conspicuously successful example, indeed a model, of what can be done in this respect. Papanoutsos's part in the language controversy, however, notable as it has been, is not within the terms of reference of this book. It is the substance of his thought with which the book is concerned.

G. P. Henderson

University of Dundee

Chronology

(Note: The books mentioned in this table are restricted to the most significant of Papanoutsos's philosophical works. Others are listed in the Bibliography.)

1900	Evangelos Panagiotou Papanoutsos born on 27 July in Piraeus.
1915–1919	Studies in theology and literature at the University of Athens.
1919	Awarded Diploma of the University of Athens.
1919–1920	Military service.
1921–1924	First period as teacher at Averoff *Gymnasion* (Greek community school) in Alexandria (Egypt).
1924–1926	Studies in philosophy, literature, and education at the Universities of Berlin, Tübingen, and Paris.
1927	Awarded Doctorate of Philosophy at the University of Tübingen.
1927–1931	Second period as teacher at Averoff *Gymnasion.*
1931–1934	Head of Teacher Training College in Mytilene (Lesbos).
1934–1944	Head of Paedagogic Academies in Alexandroupolis (Thrace), Ioannina (Epirus), Tripolis (Peloponnese), and Piraeus.
1944–1965	At intervals General Director or General Secretary at Ministry of Education in Athens. (General Director, November 1944–May 1946; January 1952–February 1953. General Secretary, June 1950–February 1951; November-December 1963; February 1964–July 1965.) Main architect of educational reform program enacted in 1956 and revived in essentials in 1976.

1946   Begins association as regular literary correspondent with Athens newspaper *To Vima* [The Rostrum]. Continued till 1967, resumed after restoration of democracy in 1974. Cofounder of Education Association *Athenaion* in Athens. Overseer of studies and regular lecturer on philosophy, psychology, and education till closure in 1967. Editor (till its cessation in 1961) of periodical *Education* (later *Education and Life*).

1948   *Aesthetics*.

1949   *Ethics*.

1953   Vol. 1 of *Modern Greek Philosophy*.

1954   *Gnosiology*.

1956   Vol. 2 of *Modern Greek Philosophy*.

1957–1958   Adviser to Government Committees on Education, and on Literature and Arts.

1958   Collaborates with K. A. Doxiadis in foundation of Athenian Technological Organization. Becomes Vice-President of Directing Council and overseer (till 1975) of Schools of Artistic and Professional Studies. *Philosophy and Education*.

1963   *Philosophical Problems*.

1965   Awarded Honorary Degree of Doctor of Laws (LL.D.) by the University of St. Andrews (Scotland).

1971   *Reason and Man*.

1974–1977   Serves in Parliament as State Deputy nominated by Center party.

1976   *State and Justice*.

1980   Elected Academician by the Academy of Athens.

1981   Appointed President of Supervisory Committee of the Research Center for Greek Philosophy at the Academy of Athens.

1982   Dies in Athens, 2 May.

Chapter One

An Educationist in the Round

One of E. P. Papanoutsos's books, published in 1965, bears the title (euphonious in Greek but not in English) *Struggles and Tribulations on behalf of Education.* As the chronological table of his life and works indicates, his long career has indeed been a continuous engagement with education, on many fronts. He has not been a university "academic." At the age of thirty-nine he renounced the idea, which he had entertained to some extent up till then, of working for a university chair. He did so partly out of distaste for the system of appointment as he had seen it, but more positively and importantly because he was conscious of a commitment to the advancement and reform of education in its widest national, and not just university, setting; and he knew well that he had it in him to produce work on his own, in philosophy and related subjects, which could be at least as scholarly, influential, and exploratory as anything which he might write from a university professor's desk.

The result of that decision has been a decisive change in the face of general Greek education, and a massive contribution to Greek "thought," together constituting a legacy to Papanoutsos's fellow countrymen which can be summed up in one word, "enlightenment." His own early experience as a teacher in Alexandria soon convinced him of the futility and inappropriateness, in many circumstances, of learning by rote. He was already beginning to see that the questioning mind, discussion, and argument—in short, the Socratic approach and mode of procedure—held out to a pupil better promise of *personal* progress, at least in many subjects, than habituated learning or drilling; and not only so,

1

but if open-mindedness is a mark of civilized behavior, then better promise also of a pupil's education being, in general, civilizing. More and more he came to see a certain symmetry in the teacher-pupil relationship: whereas the teacher undoubtedly "conveys" something to the pupil, directly or indirectly, the development and exploitation (the amendment, perhaps) of what is conveyed can depend usefully on something conveyed by the pupil to the teacher, whether a question, a request for confirmation or clarification, a suggestion, some "new idea," or the like. The values involved are those of explicitness, the real *understanding* of a principle or point of view or mode of investigation and so on, and mutual respect in the attempt to make progress with any subject of instruction or discussion, as the case may be. As Papanoutsos well recognizes, these values are indeed "ideal": this does not mean that he believes in them any the less for being so. They are part and parcel of a humanism which he has commended in the following advice to teachers of every kind: "Educate your pupils to be 'friends of man,' that is, to believe in man, to respect him and honour him—both in their neighbour's person and in their own. And let them thus discover the pride of being human."[1]

Papanoutsos steadfastly maintained his interest in the problems of educability, and his faith in the liberalizing effect of a philosophical approach to these problems, during thirteen unimaginably difficult and discouraging years, covering the Metaxas dictatorship and the Second World War, when he was in charge of various teacher-training establishments, one after another, in different parts of Greece. In spite of the frequency with which he was moved around, the poor provision of educational resources, and the general hardship of life in that period—in spite above all of the nonexistence of any satisfactory philosophical climate of opinion about education—Papanoutsos was well placed to observe and to learn. The many pupil-teachers of whom he was in charge during these years yielded him many friends in later life. Their concern with and discussions about the problems of public education had necessarily, in conditions of such stringency, been "close to the bone." But in the process Papanoutsos's educational philosophy became more and more widely known among serious students—although traduced elsewhere—and he himself gave constant thought to the problems of its application: how to provide concrete means and determine sound methods whereby education could really become the "cultivation" of the individual.

It was not until 1964 that Papanoutsos was given an opportunity seriously to tackle this problem in practice: as an overall problem for Greek education, not piecemeal; and administratively, not just in theoretical discussion, however useful. After the parliamentary election in February of that year he became for the fifth time General Secretary (or General Director—the title had varied) at the Ministry of Education. Important enough as it had been before, this time the position was crucial. Educational reform was at the apex of the new government's program; so much so that the Prime Minister, George Papandreou, himself served also as Minister of Education. Papandreou supplied authority and deep commitment, but Papanoutsos made the running as both man of ideas and chief executant of the government's policy.

The upshot, achieved phenomenally within the period of seventeen months, which was all that the Papandreou regime was vouchsafed, was a scheme of educational reform without parallel in modern Greek history and resting on a philosophy of education which would be exemplary in any setting. Public education was to be free at all levels. The terminus of compulsory education was raised from age twelve to age fifteen. New schools were established, new teachers were found, and the size of classes was reduced. Secondary education (especially) was radically replanned and special provision was made to stimulate the teaching of mathematics, physics, and foreign languages. New optional subjects were introduced. Examinations were standardized and the supply of textbooks of all kinds reviewed and greatly augmented. The training of teachers was extended and intensified. Educational administration was reorganized. Perhaps most important of all, the natural language of the people, the so-called demotic, was accorded for the first time equal status, as a medium of teaching of all kinds and at all levels from that of the nursery school to that of the university, with the so-called *katharevousa* or "purist" language which had dominated education, especially at the higher levels, since the foundation of the Greek state. The first steps were taken to found new universities, in Patras, Ioannina, and other provincial centers, whereby to relieve congestion in Athens and Salonica, and, more positively, to give these provincial centers something to live for educationally. The whole program was an application of Papanoutsos's own maxim, contained in an address which he gave to the General Assembly of UNESCO in 1964, that no country, poor any more than rich, can permit itself the luxury of indifference to the education of its youth.

The subsequent history of these reforms needs to be mentioned briefly. The program as such was annulled by the dictatorship of 1967–1974 and the progressive movement which it had initiated was put disastrously into reverse. The system of financially free education survived, as did some aspects of the new principles of selection for entry into higher education which had been part of the program; and the policy of founding new university institutions was continued. But everything essential to the style and content of education as envisaged in the reform measures of 1965 was renounced. For this reason quite apart from personal deprivations and risk, the years of the dictatorship were for Papanoutsos most unhappy. It was very difficult at that stage to see any future for the educational thinking which had engaged his mind for so long and which had taken such promising form in 1964 and 1965.

Nevertheless, the unexpected occurred. Between 1974 and 1977, during which time Papanoutsos was serving in Parliament as a State Deputy for the Center party of George Mavros, the Karamanlis government effectively revived the educational reform program of the 1960s and indeed extended it in certain directions, notably that of technical education. Throughout the process Papanoutsos, with the benefit of interparty good will in this field of public affairs at least, had a profound influence on the preparation and parliamentary discussion of the revived and revised measures. These have provided for, among other things, the introduction of demotic as the medium of instruction and of administration in elementary and secondary education, the restoration of a nine-year period of compulsory education, a reclassification of types of secondary school, a new emphasis on "professional" education, modernization of the teaching of classical culture, and the institution of a Research and Monitoring Center to look after school-educational problems of every kind. In regard to all this the inspiration and guidance of Papanoutsos have been widely recognized throughout Greece.

In its simplest terms, the philosophical point of view which has been the kernel of Papanoutsos's extended and wide-ranging educational activity has been respect for *freedom*.[2] The freedom in question is something which not even the best of educational systems can bestow on people, although it takes a good educational system to provide conditions in which that freedom can be engendered and develop. The struggle for freedom as Papanoutsos envisages it is against internal rather than external forces. It is a self-liberation which demands some little heroism, even a measure of nobility (as he puts it). The liberation is from ignorance, superstition, error—in general, from whatever can make a person "seize up" spiritually and prevent him from standing on his own feet. An educational system, however good, cannot endow him with such heroism and nobility as are needed to sustain and encourage him in overcoming the forces of darkness. What it can do is to begin to show him by example what the nature of these forces is and how, in various ways, they can be overcome. Gradually, it is to be hoped, but progressively, the individual in such circumstances will take the process of recognition and emancipation upon himself—it being an article of faith in this very Aristotelian style of thinking that some heroism and some nobility are part of our common human endowment, although all too commonly they become occluded.

That the individual, depending upon these qualities of character, should be enabled to develop a respect for reason and at the same time an enquiring and exploratory turn of mind, is the great primary objective, but not the be-all and end-all of the style of education which Papanoutsos has striven to establish. The

kind of freedom which that style of education immediately en-
courages is not for the benefit merely of the individual's powers
of reason and his store of knowledge. It becomes a facet of character, a habit and a disposition which can affect him as an entire
human being. Papanoutsos insists, indeed, that it is a necessary
condition of *moral* freedom or autonomy, which he sees as another
human ideal, again not confined in its bearing to the self-devel-
opment of the individual.[3] For he holds that moral freedom is,
in turn, a necessary condition of political freedom, regarded as
a state of affairs which rests on respect for mutuality, for tolerance
which is not indifference, and for moderation the essence of which
is having regard to the rights and claims of others.

These views represent a "philosophy of education" in a broad
and conventionally understood sense of the phrase. Does it take
a philosopher to hold them? Obviously not. They *can* be held
more or less as articles of faith, with little or no theoretic background. But if that happens they are comparatively vulnerable,
being no more proof against repudiation than any set of dogmas
that depends for its acceptance on mere preference of one kind
or another. To recommend themselves effectively they do have
to rest upon "philosophy" taken in a rather more professional
sense, so that they can be provided at need with a rationale or
justification. In the case of Papanoutsos their justification consists
in the fact that they arise out of a comprehensive view of human
nature and its possibilities that is the upshot of prolonged, scholarly, disciplined study. So that while one could write at length—
and with very good reason—about Papanoutsos's educational
achievements in the field and in government, it is also possible
to go deeper than these, into the phenomenological philosophy
which is the matrix of his whole scheme of thought and set of
values in relation to human spirituality. That is why this book
is fundamentally about Papanoutsos the philosopher, and only
for introductory purposes about Papanoutsos the educationist.

The impression must not be given, however, that there is a
sharp and arbitrary distinction to be made between these two
aspects of Papanoutsos's total personality. More often than not
one feels that in his philosophical writing he is consciously teach-

ing—albeit at this high level—as well as struggling to find answers for himself. This explains to a large extent the mode of composition and the style of his books which are, characteristically, bulky and didactic. They convey the impression that they are written partly in answer to a general social need, to "cover the ground" in philosophical subjects in which, at the time when they were written, Greek literature was strikingly defective.

For example, his *Aesthetics* (first published in 1946) is an enormous book, consisting of 440 pages of text in two type-sizes, one of them very small. As such, however, it is not atypical. The scope of the book matches its length. Its approach to the great questions of aesthetics is both historical and analytical: and from whichever of these points of view it is regarded, it succeeds in being a veritable manual of its subject. To take first the raw material of that subject: from the graphic art of primitive peoples to surrealism, from music in association with poetry, dance or religious ceremony to the self-sufficiency of the modern symphony, and correspondingly with the other main art forms, the historical "material" of aesthetics is conscientiously surveyed; so much so that, the reader may feel, there is nothing for theorizing to miss. Similar thoroughness is characteristic of the aesthetics proper on its historical side. From Plato through to a vast corpus of modern French and German aesthetic writing, with its multifarious lines of enquiry, the great questions are followed. Whether it is Aristotle, for example, or Kant or Bergson or Max Dessoir whose views are being scrutinized, the essentials are brought out carefully and clearly. Yet this historical side of the work is not done entirely for its own sake, for the record. Rather, it puts in context and gives substance to a general endeavor to bring out the nature of the classic questions in aesthetics and to answer them—an enterprise for which more recent aesthetics, by and large, has lost its nerve. The sweep is great, taking in such problems as that of aesthetic and other kinds of value, aesthetic experience, form, and content, aesthetic "emotion," aesthetic realism and idealism, and others on that plane; and more particular questions like the rationale of poetry, the peculiarities of tragedy and comedy, the role of the actor, the freedom of the architect, and so on. The fact that by 1979 about 20,000 copies of this book had been sold suggests that it has indeed answered to a felt cultural need among Greek students.

Occasionally Papanoutsos particularizes the nature of this need with which he is so concerned. He does so, for example, in his *Ethics* (first published in 1948). This volume, almost equal to *Aesthetics* in length, is even more didactic, with a larger proportion of quoted material. The prominence of this material and the general didacticism, however, are deliberate. In explaining and defending these features of his book Papanoutsos says things which are very revelatory of the character, not only of his *Ethics,* but also to some extent of his systematic philosophy in general.

The provision of philosophical literary material in our country is poor. Translations of foreign works have been scanty. And not all of them are reliable. When we write, we have a duty to consider the public which will read our books, as also the resources which it has at its disposal to enable it to follow the development of our thoughts. What is the sense in referring the reader, just in order to hasten our own progress, to authors whose language perhaps he does not know and whose works are not to be found in public libraries? For a long time to come the Greek philosophical book will be obliged to offer its readership not only the author's personal views, but also the more general educational elements that are indispensable for the understanding of these. Above all, textual passages. Many passages, from the world's philosophical legacy in general. This is an additional burden on Greek authors. And on their books.[4]

In *Ethics* particularly, Papanoutsos has followed his own advice. What stands out in that book is the great earnestness of the author's concern with the nature of moral uncertainty, and his anxiety to leave no great and forceful statement of a position, in the age-old attempt to see into and through that uncertainty, out of his own or the reader's reckoning.

The ideal of comprehensiveness is characteristic of Papanoutsos's *Gnosiology* (otherwise, *Foundations of Knowledge*) as well as of *Aesthetics* and *Ethics,* these three being the "core" books of his philosophy, and the most "systematic." Elsewhere his presentation of the subject tends to be more concentrated on special topics, or special philosophers, or to be supplementary to what he has written in the three works named. But in these works, as elsewhere, it is always Papanoutsos who is talking. He is no mere expositor, no mere "teacher of philosophy." That is why it is possible, as is done in the remainder of this book, to present his thoughts topic by topic, and take the more exegetical side of his work for granted. The full range of his grasp and scholarship will not thereby be revealed, but his own ideas about human nature and its capacity—it is to be hoped—will be.

The term "phenomenological" was applied earlier in this chapter to Papanoutsos's philosophy. Its point is this. What engrosses him primarily is how human beings take the world, what they "see" in the world, what they make of it, what prospects it holds for them, and so on. It is human *experience* of the world, whether in its necessary forms or not-so-necessary, whether receptive or creative, that he attempts primarily to portray. He is interested in "appearances" (phenomena) in this sense. He does not set himself the task of getting behind the "appearances" of human experience to an order of things that is prior to these. His philosophy is not cosmological, and it is not fundamentally metaphysical. It has affinites with empiricism, but not with the pared-down empiricism familiar to us in modern times as "positivism." It is too humanist and too wide-ranging for that. Papanoutsos does have a strong interest in psychology, and this often gives his philosophical work a distinctly psychological flavor. But the psychology involved is not that of the laboratory. It is, rather, what used to be called "analytic psychology," a subject allied to philosophy and not altogether unrelated to the "phenomenology" of experience that Continental philosophers particularly have worked on in modern times. Papanoutsos's philosophy accordingly is a deep well from which he has drawn in articulating his educational views and putting them to use.

Chapter Two
Philosophical Outlook, Style, and Method
The Critical Philosopher[1]

When Papanoutsos writes about the *critical* philosopher, he explicitly takes as his starting-point Immanuel Kant's conviction that through critical intellectual activity of a certain kind there is to be found a middle road between dogmatism and skepticism. Neither for Kant nor for Papanoutsos, however, does the middle road represent any kind of compromise between these two extremes. In the direction which it takes it owes nothing to either of them, but it is guided by criteria and ideals which are of its own and not derivative, even in the sense of being an amendment of any which either dogmatism or skepticism would recognize. The criteria and ideals in question are presented by Papanoutsos as belonging to an objectively describable type of thinker, but it is obvious that they also express his own philosophical testament, that they are values of the utmost personal significance to him. In fact we may take his account of the critical philosopher as introducing us to the general style of his own whole intellectual undertaking.

Papanoutsos first looks at various features of critical philosophy which have been highlighted by philosophical history, and, second, gives us a synoptic, and in a way more comprehensive, analysis of his own. Throughout, what he is attempting to depict is not just a certain theoretical program or theoretical cast of mind, but an attitude to truth which is in the last resort moral, an attitude the maintenance of which requires a type of character and of virtues which, rarely as they may be realized, are of an exemplary social value. They depend upon the respect for truth, and they concern themselves about truth; but in so doing they reveal that morally significant character out of which alone such respect and concern can issue.

The intellectual probing, examination, and testing of received opinion, carried out strictly, watchfully, and methodically, is a philosophical style and pursuit due above all to Socrates. This style principally, Papanoutsos observes, gave its initial impetus to critical philosophy. In its background was the consideration that, when moved to attempt to understand, correlate, and in general makes sense of prevailing beliefs in various fields, an enquiring mind could find itself in either of two positions: it could lapse hopelessly into skepticism or it could undertake a radical review of the code or codes examined. The first of these outcomes (Papanoutsos would certainly wish to hold) is faint hearted; the second, resolute. Doubt is what we begin with, and doubt or uncertainty is what we may be left with. But there is a world of difference between "terminal" doubt and the uncertainty which, in a curiously optimistic way, goes on with the analysis of concepts and the construction and testing of theories, moved by respect for truth but expecting, in its questings, perhaps no more than an approximation to truth. In this connection, Socrates expected relatively little; others, like Descartes, more. But Socratic and Cartesian alike, while moved by doubt, have been able to live with doubt in the sense that they have recognized it as a continual stimulus and never abandoned themselves to it. So too with Papanoutsos.

Is critical philosophy, however, doomed to be a more or less unsuccessful attempt at a resolution of questions without limit? Not altogether, it has been argued. Are there not some questions which we can refuse? Kant's great contribution to critical philosophy was, in effect, to raise (or reraise) this question. Some kinds of apparently posable questions, questions for example about God, freedom, immortality, and the world behind the appearances with which, in our everyday experiences, we have to do, are "questions" that theoretical reason must simply put into suspension. In arguing thus, however, Kant saw himself as delineating various great classes of question with which theoretical reason could fairly hope to make some progress. The critical spirit, with this particular concentration of its enquiries upon the "organ" and the possible resources of knowledge, achieved, as Papanoutsos claims, a new maturity and decisiveness; and, as he indicates, Kant thus contrived to discipline it against a great variety of possible dogmatisms.

By tradition, Papanoutsos says, critical philosophy is a *dialectical* style of thought. "It loves dialogue, it is accomplished by dialogue, it is nourished by dialogue."[2] Taken in application to Descartes and Kant, this might seem a strange observation, and the remark, which he makes later, that "the critical philosopher is essentially one who engages in dialogue, not monologue"[3] might seem embarrassing in this connection. But Papanoutsos hastens to explain that dialogue can be a mode of personal as well as of interpersonal philosophizing. What is essential to it is not the crude confrontation, as it were, of consideration and counterconsideration, but "elucidation, development, the achievement of greater adequacy for each term [in a process of thinking] in a context where it is subject to [intellectual] conflict, and by having it come up against and stand in contradistinction to others."[4] He adds that a dialectical spirit, and hence critical philosophy as such, can flourish only where there is freedom of thought and expression. This consideration, he thinks, both stands to reason and can be seen by a methical study of social history.

What style of individual then, is the critical philosopher who thus engages in dialogue, either with others or with himself? To begin with, he must be impelled by a passion for knowledge: he is a theorist *par excellence,* one who displays (as Papanoutsos puts it so picturesquely) "sense in the service of intellect, perception suffused by thought, language as being one with reflection, *Logos.*"[5] Along with the passion for knowledge goes a consciousness of responsibility. The critical philosopher feels that a man can engage in no more sacred mission than the quest for truth; consequently, superficiality and haste in embracing a view are anathema to him, as is the whole idea of making intellectual play out of questions of moment. Papanoutsos puts a moral construction on this attitude. The failings just mentioned amount to "a lack of self-respect, a moral lapse."[6] Rectitude in the pursuit of truth is, it seems, a moral as well as an intellectual virtue.

Then, the critical philosopher is temperamentally also a man apart. His spirit is markedly philanthropic. There is no question of his adopting variable standards in his assessment of what mortal men hold to, whether in their more particular beliefs about the world or in their general theorizings or in subscription to moral, political, or religious principles—or any other kind of principle. The same austere standards of judgment must prevail throughout. But recognizing how *difficult* intellectual endeavor is, how hard to practice is authenticity in any of its modes, he proffers his judgments in clemency. He himself has chosen the hard road, on which the problematic has to be recognized and overcome at every stage. If others have chosen likewise he respects them and their judgments accordingly; if they have not followed his own hard route, but through deficiencies in ability or training, or perhaps because of the practical exigencies of life have foreclosed on certain theoretical or practical options, they may still be due credit for integrity in that their choices have been honorably made. They may be in error, but they are not, as such, ill-doers. Indeed it is never safe to assume, as a reflection upon the personal character of an individual, the apparent ill-judgedness of his choices or beliefs.

Circumspection is another virtue which has one foot in the moral, the other in the intellectual domain. On both sides, but particularly the second, it is also a virtue of the critical philosopher. Descartes construed it in terms of his famous "clearness and distinctness" principle, involving a solemn injunction against yielding to "precipitancy and prejudice" in judgment. Papanoutsos construes it rather more in a Kantian fashion, in terms of a constant sensitivity to the possible bounds of human knowledge, and a constant willingness to recognize that upon some classes of apparent "questions" the circumspect philosopher will simply refrain from pronouncing. He will do so not through intellectual timorousness, but out of a reasoned conviction that there are limits to the kinds of "questions" which human intelligence can tackle; that is, to which it can address itself with any prospect of a reasonably grounded answer. In this particular context, Papanoutsos does not indicate how these limits are drawn; but he remarks on the misplaced expectations with which people are accustomed to look to philosophy for answers to hallowed metaphysical or religious forms of "question," and on the disappointment or positive disapproval with which philosophical circumspection in these matters may be met.

Fifth, and last, the critical philosopher will be possessed of philosophic courage. This is partly a matter of sheer perseverance in the work of philosophical investigation and analysis; more strikingly, perhaps, it is the philosopher's ability to maintain his position and his discipline, and pursue his aims, without concession to ideologies or "enthusiasms." Such fortitude may be difficult. There is comfort to be found in the role of follower or adherent; and unpopularity, again, may be the reward of a refusal to participate in "movements," sponsor "causes," belong to such and such a "school," and so on. No doubt Papanoutsos would allow the critical philosopher, as a man of flesh and blood, to have his loyalties; but here, as elsewhere, as in his life-style in general, the philosopher will be circumspect.

What manner of man, then, have we here? Someone, it may seem, very like David Hume, who comes irresistibly to the author's mind in this connection. Hume indeed had a passion for knowledge, a sense of intellectual responsibility, a philanthropic spirit, rational circumspection, and philosophic courage. Perhaps the main difference between Hume and Papanoutsos's "ideal" critical philosopher would have been Hume's love of literary fame, his "ruling passion" as he himself confesses. The critical philosopher is ruled by the need to pursue the truth, rather than by any glory in communicating the truth.

Dialectical Method

Forms of Dialectic.[7]   It will be apparent from the preceding section that there is a close connection in Papanoutsos's mind between the notion of a philosophical dialogue and that of dialectic, as a method or procedure of discursive thought. A more direct account of his concept of dialectic is, therefore, now required.

He first of all puts forward a series of basic properties ascribable to dialectical relationships (i.e., relationships susceptible of a dialectical philosophical development), taken as holding between pairs of problematic terms. The later of these properties presuppose the earlier, and present increasing complexity. The properties are (1) Reciprocity: a general "confrontation," or need to take account of one another, of two different terms occurring at the same level of enquiry. (2) Conflict: a stage beyond the reciprocal difference of two terms as formulated above. A certain clash of intention as between the two terms is now involved. (3) Dynamic alternation: the attraction and repulsion of two terms occurring as above in conflict at the same level of enquiry.

It has to be confessed that the account of dialectical properties thus summarized is abstract and schematic. The notion of "a term" needs elucidation; it is not explained what constitutes "the same level of enquiry"; no examples are given of any of the three properties named; and the metaphor, "attraction and repulsion," is left to speak for itself. Ironically, the only example broached is one which fails to satisfy the criteria of a dialectical relationship. Suppose it be suggested that there is such a relationship between the concepts of beauty and of utility (or inutility for that matter). These terms do *not* determine a field of forces such as is indicated in (3) above. For there is no necessary tension (attraction and repulsion) between them in all possible circumstances; and, since the one represents an aesthetic, the other a practical value, it is only fortuitously, as Papanoutsos puts it, that they encounter one another in the same field of reference.

The relationship of beauty and utility is thus only apparently dialectical: in the light of the above considerations the "problem" which they present is dissolved rather than solved. Another way of dissolving an apparently dialectical relationship is to show that the terms involved are not naturally, but only artificially, in dialectical relationship; so that any synthesis of their opposition which is attempted is itself artificial. This is what happens,

Papanoutsos thinks, in the Kantian attempt to bring together the opposing ideas of psychological and of moral freedom. You can only work these ideas into a dialectical synthesis if you impoverish them unendurably. And then there is no real "synthesis." How can a will be free (psychologically undetermined) and at the same time subject to a law (that of the moral conscience)? The impoverishment involved seems to consist in turning each of the two terms, the will and the law, into a limiting case. "Only a will which is always ready to sacrifice its independence to its moral aspirations could be reconciled with the notion of a law which issues its decrees without restricting the freedom of its votaries. But such a will is as minimally free (in the full sense of the term) as the corresponding law is to be deemed [maximally authoritative, i.e.] absolute."[8] The example is a difficult one, but its point appears to be that it shows itself defective because it fails to exhibit property (3), dynamic alternation—the emphasis being on "alternation." There can be no come-and-go between such extremes.

So far, so negative. What does Papanoutsos have to say about "positive" forms of dialectical relationship, positive (or fruitful) in that they provide material for a genuine philosophical "solution" to the problem they engender, one in which justice is done to the force of each of the terms involved? He suggests that there are two such forms.

In the first, the analytical development of the terms concerned brings out a fundamental complementarity of the one to the other and does not preserve any diehard opposition between them. This procedure, as it were, "closes" the problematic aspect of the situation. A familiar example is provided by the ancient argument between realism and idealism. Here we begin with a confrontation between two theses, (1) that "reality" (whatever it is that we know or have to do with in our dealings with the world) is self-existent, *en soi,* and (2) that "reality" exists precisely inasmuch as it is something apprehended by a mind. The apparent opposition involved here, however, is really just that of two bearings taken upon the one question. The first is taken from the domain of action and perception; the second, from that of theory. Looked at in the first way, the world is there to be taken into account; we come up against it. Looked at in the second, where what operates is the intellect with all its contrivances, forms, methodical procedures, and so on, the world is nothing if not intellectually penetrated; an object of interpretation. There is much more to be said in elaboration of these two complementary points of view; but Papanoutsos is satisfied that they *are* complementary, and that what remains to be done in connection with them is a matter of detail. He says, almost wistfully, that such discoveries of complementarity, while being enlightening, are also not altogether welcome as putting the mind to rest. "The great spiritual enemy is immobility."[9]

The second form of "positive" dialectical relationship is to be contrasted with that just described, as "open" to "closed." The complementarity of terms or standpoints was something more or less latent which, once disclosed, settled the issue on the level, so to speak, on which it began. The discovery with which we are now concerned is not like this. It is a discovery of the possibility, the fruitful possibility, of *metathesis* or transformability of content, such that the "dynamic alternation" of the two factors can be dealt with in a progressively more satisfactory way as each is transposed into, or superseded by, some new conceptual form. There is no promise here of "closure," an end to the process of dialectical development. The prospect is rather that of seeing how little elementary, really, was the problem with which we began, and how it is possible to deal with it in an indefinite series of fresh ways, each adding to the grasp and interest which the problem is capable of yielding, but none constituting a strict solution to it.

An example is imperative. Fortunately Papanoutsos provides one. Consider the traditional philosophical preoccupation with the relationship between experience and reason. How are we to come to terms with this relationship? Certainly it is one which exhibits alternation, with different philosophical schools giving priority, in their constructon of theories of knowledge, now to experience and now to reason. If its emphasis is on the sheer objectivity of empirical detail, a theory (Papanoutsos suggests) will set less store on the *organizational* aspect of knowledge: on the other hand, the more it is preoccupied with the completeness and perfection of the logical side of things, the more constricted will be its view of what experience provides. Each side seeks a certain independence of the other, and yet it cannot do without the other. This state of affairs leads to an indefinitely expansive development of the problem, of which Papanoutsos gives the following account:

The two terms [*experience* and *reason*] find themselves in dialectical opposition first of all at the level of *representation*, in a context of intuitively structured *ensembles*. However, once the empirical elements become enriched by the progress of observation, so that the relatively feeble associative ordering of the data is upset, the conflict is transferred to the level of *concepts*. Here again the situation changes readily; concepts are formed ever more numerously, and the mind, to control them, organizes them within the framework of an *idea*, that is to say, a scientific hypothesis which explains a determinate class of phenomena. At a still higher level is located the *system*, where the mind, to become master of an extending range of knowable material, contrives to construct a conceptual complex that is both highly organized and well founded upon a determinate sector of reality—in other words, a special science. It might be suggested that the limiting level in this progression would be that of a *universal* system, capable of embracing and organizing all other systems in one. Such an undertaking, however, would seem to be beyond our limited human powers. [10]

It appears to the author, if he may make so mischievous a suggestion, that most of the game here is played by reason in its opponent's half. It is fairly clear that the alternation which takes place between two dialectically related terms does not have to be symmetrical—at any rate at this, that, or the next phase of the history of opposition between them. More will be made of this point later, however, in discussion of more concrete examples, in Papanoutsos's thinking, of the dialectical motif in philosophy. The question will also have to be borne in mind how generally this very abstract account of dialectic, and of its approvable forms, applies in philosophy—how much of philosophy is illuminated by thinking of it thus in dialectical terms.

Thought in Dialectical Progression. In *Philosophical Problems*[11] there are available three usefully concrete examples to illustrate the "open" type of dialectical progression of which such a formal account was given in *Philosophy and Education*. The first comes from the domain of what may be called historicosociology. It concerns the question "What is the contribution of colonization to human development, economic and cultural?" The second belongs to biology, and has to do with the question what scope there is, in the study of animals and of plants, for the recognition of transmissible, but acquired, specific characteristics. The third is a matter of conceptual analysis, where the question is: "How are the terms (concepts) *rivalry* [or *emulation, amilla*] and *antagonism* related to one another in point of significance? Do they coincide or is one [wholly or partially] exclusive of the other?" It can be taken that the three examples are chosen not only as clear illustrations of contexts in which progress is made dialectically, but also for their variety—so as to suggest that in looking at human thinking in dialectical terms one is bringing out a natural and pervasive feature of it, and neither distorting it nor making too much out of a spasmodic kind of intellectual exercise. An account will be given of the first example only—like the others it is professedly simple and neither technical nor esoteric— but it will be noted how Papanoutsos sees in all three the outstanding characteristics of "open" dialectical progression.

We begin with an uncompromising-looking but quite familiar position, taken in answer to the question raised about the benefits of colonization. (This will be the "thesis.") Let it be suggested that colonization, by and large, *is* an element of progress both for the country which experiences it and for humankind generally. Typically (the thesis would have it), the colonizer will bring to the colonized benefits both technological and cultural which have become features of a more "advanced" society and which, left to itself, the colonized community could not hope to achieve. Now the first thing that will occur to a reflective recipient of this suggestion is the number of relevant possibilities which it ignores, notably (1) rapacity and rough treatment which the colonized are liable to suffer at the hands of the colonizer, (2) haphazard and damaging exploitation, by the colonizer, of natural resources, and (3) estrangement of the colonized from their indigenous civilization. And the second thing that will strike him, unfavorably, is the sheer assumption (4) that the colonizer is indispensable in various ways to the progress of the colonized. Might not the colonized, in the end of the day, do better by their own efforts, exerted perhaps slowly but with more secure results?

It would be hard for these blemishes not to produce doubts in the mind of the proponent of the thesis. His immediate response, however, might be to represent his position as if it could comprehend and allow for the demurrers listed. The effect would be to give it a more compromising appearance, along the following lines. "In spite of possibility (1), even allowing for possibility (2), and acknowledging possibility (3), colonization is nevertheless an element of progress. As to (4), there is really a positive disadvantage in the delay envisaged." This version when filled out is an improvement on the original if only as taking more factors into account. But it is difficult to stay with. One objection tends to suggest, perhaps to be supported by, another; and the expanse of uncertainty grows. In other words, an antithesis takes shape: in the process, the etiology of the antithesis is worked out and elaborated. Colonization, one may now suggest, is not after all an element of progress. It involves historical discontinuities, physical and moral, which are good neither for colonized nor for colonizer. "At best"—Papanoutsos thinks of the objector as saying—"colonization is a means of spreading a formalized conformity in modes of expression, in methods of thought and production, in manners and in ideas, which stifles people's creative urge and impoverishes human history."[12]

In the antithesis thus adumbrated the types of discontinuity noted in the first part would be worked out as elaborations of the initial stances (1), (2), (3), and (4) taken against the thesis. But more is involved in the antithesis than just that. The idea of a "formalized conformity" is a new and important factor in the discussion. Even if it does have some pragmatic or logical connection with ideas which have already figured in the discussion, the connection has been of the most implicit, so that we now have an important extension of the terms of reference of our argument. The antithesis is not just a simple, point-by-point denial of the original thesis, but involves something "further." In this very development, however, the antithesis itself is now "exposed," in the following fashion. "*Is* it indeed the case that the formation and spread of a unitary, ecumenical civilization, which undoubtedly will deepen and grow roots as time goes on, represents a loss, historically regarded . . . or is it rather a success which will open the way to new achievements?"[13] This question brings the whole discussion into a new focus. We can, of course, throw up our hands in despair at such complication, and return to the original thesis (or to a point-blank denial of it). Alternatively, we can welcome the opportunity which it gives us to exercise ourselves on the antithesis (at which we have arrived) of the original antithesis, and thereby to occupy, for however short or long a time, a more or less hard-won new position, an improved "thesis" on a higher level of sophistication.

In this example, the notion of "formalized conformity," which was a factor in the original antithesis, played the part of a catalyst. In his biological examples, Papanoutsos shows how a correspondingly crucial difference is made by the introduction, into controversy about inherited characteristics, of the idea that there can be an "evolution of species" that is without limitation and, as he puts it, "always open in every direction."[14] This principle, too, is vulnerable; but it, too, enables us to make progress in sophistication. Similarly with the meaning-analysis of *rivalry* and *antagonism:* the catalyst here is the insistence that in rivalry there are (ineliminable) elements of magnanimity, scrupulosity, and respect for other contenders which put an absolute barrier between it and antagonism. Again we are presented with a consideration which is both vulnerable and fertile.

In all three examples, the original thesis was overselective: it picked on and fitted together various aspects of a problematic situation neatly enough, but it left lacunas which for a questing mind became positive stimuli for the construction of a counterpoise. The counterpoise, however, had to be persuasive. It had to avoid overselectiveness in its turn, and it had to summon such support as would both take account of the thesis and put it in context. On the other hand, these corrective considerations, as Papanoutsos puts it, "work cumulatively: they call in aid much more numerous and more suggestive elements than would suffice simply to provide a foundation for the antithesis, and by this 'overstepping' they give the new constructon . . . [in turn] an unstable balance."[15] But this is progress. Progressive approximations to a solution of a problem bring about *understanding*. It would be quite misleading merely to think of them as perpetual failures finally to solve that problem.

It will be noted that Papanoutsos adverts more than once to the fact that, in the examples which he provides, the antithesis is more than a mere denial, point by point, of the thesis. It needs a "foundation": it must have its rationale. But one must note also Papanoutsos's emphasis on the way in which, in the presentation of the antithesis, a new and exploitable consideration emerges. The reader may experience some uncertainty at such points. What are the criteria according to which a consideration *is* emergent, and not just part of the minimal "foundation" of the antithesis? Presumably even a minimally founded antithesis (however one should describe this) would not be completely infertile. Too much precision, however, should not be expected in this context. Papanoutsos's examples do show us that, in one way or another, an energetically pursued counterargument does turn up considerations which keep an intellectual enquiry on the move. What sort of considerations do this best will vary very much from case to case. If the original thesis is merely elliptical, an antithesis will have to aim at comprehensiveness, among other things. If it is distorted or exaggerated, an antithesis will have to aim at a certain pointedness. We should note, however, that these two defects (and the corresponding aims) are not altogether independent of one another.

Genuine Dialogue.[16] In raising the question as to what constitutes a genuine dialogue, Papanoutsos in effect returns to the idea of the critical philosopher. About the critical philosopher's discourse there is an openness which differentiates it utterly from that of the eristic, or merely disputatious man. What sort of openness? Well, first of all the critical philosopher does not seek to indulge in monologue: he is receptive or open to whatever reasoned considerations a participant in discussion may put to him. More importantly for present purposes, though, he exposes what he himself has to say to the possibility of fair objection on whatever grounds. His motive for doing so is not that of entering into an intellectual contest and "taking on" an opponent so as to corner and beat him. It is as far as possible removed from that. Nor—and this is an interestingly contrasting consideration—is it that of reaching agreement, at all costs, upon the problem at issue. What matters is how, and how far, he and his interlocutors can progress toward a possible agreement. In other words, the methodology of the proceedings matters! Consequently what he would urge is not that people "should 'arrive' in any event at agreement with the interlocutor who maintains an opinion different from their own (this would be odd; someone who takes a methodical part in dialogue isn't a teacher of good behavior . . .), but that they should smooth out as well as they can the road which 'might possibly lead to agreement' with him, even if in the end this agreement does not come about."[17]

The second feature of critical openness, namely the exposure of what one has to say to fair comment, requires further elucidation. Papanoutsos undertakes this in the first place by asking what it is that occludes someone's position in discussion, what sort of things prevent him from meeting, in genuine rational encounter, some more or less different point of view. What Papanoutsos has in mind, he explains, is not the psychological factors which may lie behind a person's inability or unwillingness to "show his hand" in discussion and argument, but the logical and semantic characteristics of the situation in which this happens. Papanoutsos highlights two sets of these characteristics, by means of an example which, familiar and elementary though it may seem initially, turns out to be susceptible to considerable development and elaboration. "Does the world make progress or not?"

The first and most obvious way in which a satisfactory understanding, on how to handle and get on with this question, can fail to be achieved, is through lack of definition of terms. What "world" are we talking about? And, supposing we reach some agreement on that, what would it be for such a world to "progress"? Various possibilities which, in each instance, we have to take into account suggest themselves readily. Papanoutsos rehearses them in some detail, and it is not necessary here to follow him in doing so. The main point is that lack of definition simply fails to provide an initial context in which discussion can proceed to any advantage, in which (that is) there can be any meeting of minds in rational respects.

The second way in which a satisfactory understanding can fail to be achieved is less obvious and less easy to describe, but presents just as real an obstacle as the first. Supposing we do come to an agreement as to what exactly we are to mean by the terms *world* and *progress,* we can still be in an impasse. "If I present their logical relationship," Papanoutsos says, "in the very simple form S—P, where the only terms to figure are the given two, formulated without elaboration, I leave my opposing interlocutor no leeway in which to move; all he can do is reject my opinion in a similar curt and categorical fashion."[18] The difficulty, presumably, is that since the two terms are not definitionally elaborated (even in the way in fact agreed), the relationship between them cannot be elaborated (the nature of this elaboration being not as yet agreed). It can be only of a crude "is—isn't" form.

What, then, is required? Papanoutsos answers that the propositions in conflict must be given "nuances,"[19] and by this he does not apparently mean that they incorporate a *definiens* for a *definiendum* as agreed in stage one. He appears to be saying that, granted the meaning of *world* and granted the meaning of *progress* as settled so far, one must now venture to say something about the manner in which those terms apply. One may suggest, for example, that the world is progressing slowly, or irregularly, or in some aspects, or from a collective rather than an individual point of view, etc.; or, if and to the extent that conditions (1), (2), (3), and (4) are all operative, or inasmuch as (1)—e.g., economic development—coincides with (2)—e.g., medical progress or moral well-being—etc. Such qualifications represent the beginnings of concessions to a point of view opposite to that initially proposed. Clearly, one concession would tend to lead to another; but also, not all such concessions need be on one side of the argument!

Progress through a willingness to open up a dialogue is not, of course, automatic or self-guaranteeing once begun. For example, discussion about the world's progression may reach a stage at which a question arises as to the relative status of the "material" and the "spiritual" (or "cultural") aspects of civilization. Do they go hand in hand; or does one have priority over another as cause to effect? The very question is constricting. As Papanoutsos hints, we have to exert ourselves to see that there is no simple, linear connection between either one and the other, and that in assessing the general state and/or improvement of mankind at any given phase we have to be prepared to take into account an increasing complex of necessary and sufficient conditions, some of which may aptly be described in "material" terms, others in "cultural", but none of which need be given a once-for-all, nonrevisable description in this set of terms rather than that, or be assigned a priority, in explanatory power, which will not be open to question for a critical mind.

This concludes the introductory account of Papanoutsos's views about the nature, the importance and the range of dialectical reasoning. The initial abstractness in their presentation, which was noted, has been counteracted in subsequent contexts by a fair variety of examples, the tendency of which is to show that dialectic, as Papanoutsos understands it, is the essential fabric of good reasoning, and not just a method employed here and there as the occasion may demand. So far, the discussion which has been considered has been *about* dialectic. In the following chapters an attempt will be made to show, among other things, how Papanoutsos himself *uses* dialectic for his own philosophical purposes. It is to be hoped that in the process the nature of dialectic as such may become progressively clearer.

Chapter Three

Theory of Knowledge

The Ontological Problem

Three Concepts of the Subjective.[1]   What Papanoutsos regards as the nature and scope of a "theory of knowledge" will be discussed later. At this stage it is sufficient to note that such a theory, for him, is very broad, taking in the great traditional philosophical question of the relation between being and consciousness of being, classified in Papanoutsos's scheme as an (indeed the) "ontological" problem. This question involves, radically, discussion of the general confrontation between realism and idealism; and that in turn requires discussion of various ways of construing the relationship between "subject" and "object" so as to try to determine how, in the end of the day, being (fundamental being) is to be regarded. In the subsection entitled "Analysis and Synthesis" Papanoutsos's general and considered solution of this problem will be reviewed, after stock has been taken in the next subsection of his essential preliminary assessment of the scope and limits of the realist and the idealist outlooks. The aim of the present section is to show him as clearing the ground for further discussion. He does so by indicating, in dialectical fashion, how in relation to various different ways of taking the human "subject," realist and idealist tendencies set in, and how a certain clarity in this regard can save us from premature perplexity, perhaps hopelessness, about the prospects of solving the basic ontological problem.

If we start by looking at realism and idealism out of context, as it were, we are sure to put the enquiry on to the wrong lines. "When they [i.e., extreme realism and idealism] formulate the perplexity [*aporia*]: 'Does the subject constitutively determine the object, or is it constitutively determined by it?', they presuppose that the subject is one thing (in form and significance), and the object likewise, so that there is only one answer to the question. . . ."[2] In answering, we are expected to take our choice of the two alternatives posed; no third possibility is offered. Progress with the question will not be made unless we take a more careful look at what is meant by *subject* and what by *object*. Let us concentrate, therefore, on three possible concepts of "a subject" (the expectation being that corresponding concepts of "an object" will emerge correlatively).

The first is termed by Papanoutsos *psychophysiological*. He is thinking here, in a deliberately restricted fashion, of what used to be called "the embodied self." "We" here are represented by and coextensive with what our bodies do in interaction with their environment. "We" are involved, absorbed, lost in such transactions (much like Sartre's peeper through a keyhole who does not "come to himself "—as we might say—until he suddenly becomes aware that he is under scrutiny by another). The horizon of "our" world is the horizon of "our" body's actions, attempts at action and reactions. "We" may "live," strain at, savor, or otherwise emotionally experience what we do, and like or loathe what is done to us, but that is as far as we go in the direction of self-awareness. In fact, Papanoutsos suggests, this stage is "presubjective."[3] It is also, strictly speaking, preobjective; for the subject-object distinction has not yet emerged. Consequently, in relation to this level it makes no sense to raise the question whether being is in some way prior to consciousness or consciousness to being even though "we" are one with our physical and physiological world (so that there may be some temptation to think of that world as a determinant).

What we have here is not really one of three concepts of "a subject"—Papanoutsos's discussion-heading is misleading in this respect—but rather one of three contexts in which the concept of subjectivity can be looked at, the result being a *négatité* (something conspicuous by its absence) and not any positively identifiable term. Moreover, it is difficult to decide to what this account of "experience," given in psychophysiological terms, applies. Papanoutsos takes stock of various psychological studies in this area, and indicates that the account may be importantly illuminative for child psychology and possibly the psychology of some primitive or limited forms of adult human experience. But obviously, in relation to ordinary human cogitative and practical life, it is abstract and partial. Why then does Papanoutsos make so much of it as he does? The answer is probably that he sees this context of discussion as a foil against which his second approach to the subject-object relationship can be the better developed. If we cannot identify at this first level the two "poles of knowledge,"[4] we can by means of the description given anticipate, with some urgency, their emergence, and discern the possibility of a sharp relationship between them being exhibited at a higher level of enquiry.

Let us, therefore, proceed to this higher level and consider the second concept of "a subject." The motive factor in the account is now *consciousness* which is also *self*-awareness. We are thinking of a stage at which all the difference has been made by the accumulation of experience, the elaboration of action, diversified success and frustration, and the development of reflection, within that monophysite, circumscribed whole with which our account began. What has come into the reckoning and become more and more polarized is "experience" taking form as an *ego* to whom, in particular, things happen and whose initiatives have some importance in determining *what* happens. Boundaries between "the inner" and "the outer" have now been clearly established. On the one hand there is a center of reference to which is ascribable an indefinite series of functions of a certain kind—although what constitutes that kind may be highly problematic—and a corresponding series of "contents"—images, judgments, emotions, impulses, and so on. On the other hand there is an indefinitely expansive context, "things" in all their conformations including our own organically functioning bodies, and "others" taken not only as "physical" but also as "psychical" beings; all of which constitute the ego's field of reckoning and, in certain respects, its own measure.

What makes up this ("external") context is what we tend to call "the world." That is, Papanoutsos explains, "being as endowed with limits and order, being as the *practical* and *social* man of so-called common sense apprehends it, and as the *positive* sciences of the *macrocosm* take it to be: a sequence of phenomena governed by certain ascertainable and formulable laws."[5] There is no suggestion here—the contrary, rather—that natural laws are anything but the sinews of nature. On the other hand, of course, the thinking processes of the self-conscious subject also have their "texture": they are amenable to the laws of psychology and, in a different way, those of logic. The question thus arises how "the world," structured as it is in one way, can be accessible to, be known by, the self-conscious subject, structured as he is in another way. The answer, which Papanoutsos takes to be characteristic of the level of enquiry being examined, is that we have to do here with a "perhaps restricted but, within its limits, important 'pre-established harmony' or identify of principles."[6] What sort of principles these could be is not suggested. But the imagery on which this style of thought trades is that of mirroring or reflection. The self-conscious subject achieves success in acting upon and getting to know "the world" because *somehow* his own disciplined order of thought "reflects the general lawfulness of the universe."[7]

Papanoutsos himself remarks that there is an unsatisfactory ambivalence in representing a subject-object relationship in terms such as have just been used. The distinction has been established, as sharply as possible, between consciousness and whatever reality consciousness encounters. The relationship *is* one of encounter and not of interpenetration (so to speak) of reality by consciousness. To this extent the thinking involved is dualist and realist both; realist in that consciousness maintains a respectful distance between itself and that which it is consciousness *of!* But, whether all consciousness is self-consciousness or not, there *is* self-consciousness. "The world," regarded as the object of consciousness, does and does not include consciousness, it would seem. If it does, what is consciousness's mode of knowledge of itself ? Can it maintain a respectful distance between itself and itself, or is there here a special mode of awareness, a special way of taking account of something, which realism as such has missed?

Papanoutsos does not pursue these questions in the present context; nor will the author. He himself is concerned particularly to expose the realist emphasis which is natural to his second level of representation of the subject-object relationship. Summarily, we are asked to take for consideration a confrontation between two terms of knowledge, a really "existent" ego connected in the activity of knowing with a really "existent" thing. The main principle involved is that this really "existent" thing, however simple or complex a form it may take, is ontologically independent of the consciousness which strives to get to know it. Even, however, if the phenomenon of self-consciousness can somehow be reconciled with the terms of this principle, the principle itself tells us nothing about the extent to which consciousness can achieve knowledge of the independent reality which it purports to be investigating. And in this situation there is tension, from the point of view of maintaining the very realism which level two of this investigation has brought to the forefront.

For what reason? Papanoutsos draws attention to the fact that the question just raised, about the extent to which consciousness *can* have access to an "objective" world at which it sets itself, complicates the situation and puts realism itself on trial. There is a spectrum of answers to the question. They extend from the uncritical response of common-sense realism that there is, in principle, no limitation on access, by consciousness, to the "real" world with which it purports to deal, through various kinds of "critical" realism according to which "being is presented to consciousness, but only *in part*,"[8] to agnosticism, represented most notably by the views of Immanuel Kant. What Papanoutsos makes of this situation, opening up as it does a vast field of philosophical doubt, is best conveyed in his own terms. Speaking about Nikolai Hartmann's views about the difficulties of realism, but taking these views as having a general validity, he says:

They show that within every critically-illuminated realistic position there is a basic element of agnosticism. This element diminishes to a considerable extent the distance that separates realism from an idealistic stance. By acknowledging a complete or all-but-complete lack of congruence between the principles of consciousness and the laws of being, we are, in a manner, preparing our minds for the idea that in the last analysis being can be considered not as something external, to be got at, but as something which belongs internally to the articulation of thought. Thus from the depths of realism we are made to take a dialectical leap into idealism.[9]

How can "being," the *object* of our intellectual strivings, belong internally to the articulation of thought? This query brings us to the third level at which Papanoutsos presents an interpretation of the subject-object relationship. The level now is that of *pneuma:* mind or pure intellect (the word is impossible to translate satisfactorily). There is something of the same embarrassment in talking about "a subject" at this level as there was at the psychophysiological. There the "subject" was not yet separated out: here it is transcended, in such a way as to become, again, one with "its" context. But the context has now, via the second subject-object level, been dialectically transformed. Or, to vary the metaphor, it has been twice developed. In the first set of circumstances the level of personal existence had not yet been reached—the context was in one way impersonal; in the second, personal existence was shown as emergent and as enriched in various ways by its mastery and exploitation of positive knowledge of its "world"; in this, the third, setting personal existence is left behind so that the context again becomes, though in a radically different way, impersonal. Here the "subject" is, as Papanoutsos puts it, "transformed into purely intellectual authority, given over completely to one activity and one only: the theoretical."[10] The "subject" is the exerciser of a discipline, of an organized system of rules and conditions which constitute intellectual life, and which are there to be served rather than exploited; except that, of course, it is the thinking mind which gives them their vitality and which may change or develop them. This discipline, essentially, is no more for oneself than for others, or for others than oneself. The "subject" has become intersubjective!

What now of the correlative "object"? The world that is "investigated" and studied has now become, in a sense, suffused by mind. Mind is no longer subservient to nature in that it waits upon nature to suggest to it what is "true of " nature, and how the various truths which it "discovers" can most naturally be ordered and combined. On this intellectual plane, as Papanoutsos puts it "the object . . . is fashioned out of the subject's own substance. . . . It has lost its 'materiality,' that tone of 'externality' which in the preceding stage made consciousness feel it to be alien and apart from itself, and it has become conceptual in nature, a sequence of concepts, an order of concepts, rule, principle, system."[11] Of course this leaves us with a problem of interpretation, in that it has to be decided (not once for all but continuously) which range and which structures of concepts are the most appropriate to this, that and the next field of enquiry—and, indeed, what the term "appropriateness" in these circumstances means. But that is another problem. Papanoutsos's insistence is that the intellectual level which he is describing is not itself a "mere" intellectual construct. It is exemplified in much modern science, and most outstandingly in modern physics. And it clearly can be regarded as a kind of idealization of the world, nature, the objects of knowledge, as these were understood at less developed levels of enquiry.

So this is where idealism gets its footing. What Papanoutsos has done, in the present part of his work, has been to argue that the antithesis of realism and idealism should not be treated as a brute confrontation, which it can be our ambition to settle definitively, by context-regardless philosophical considerations. Instead, realism and idealism should be taken—so far as this argument goes—as points of view which emerge naturally, one in respect to one level in the development and sophistication of mind, the other at another. In a sense they—and their tension—will always be with us, because we are not beings on one level: we operate in one of our aspects with one kind of "objectivity," in another with another. But in showing where these aspects belong and what is most characteristic of them, Papanoutsos has attempted to "talk out" the tension between the two great philosophical attitudes which he regards as posing the primary ontological problem.

The Impact of the Three-Concept Analysis.[12] What was introduced in the last section as Papanoutsos's "clearing the ground for further discussion" turned out to be more than that. The description makes his analysis of the three concepts of subjectivity sound less far-reaching and comprehensive than it is. The further discussion that takes us to his "critical solution of the ontological problem" is really rather a short step. It consists essentially of a gloss on the work just done, so that there shall remain no possibility of misinterpreting its results. First we need to look at what he sometimes calls the "monolithic" nature of realism and idealism as they have occurred characteristically in the history of philosophy. What is interesting about Papanoutsos's own position is his attempt to *understand* realism and idealism, and to concede to them what they are due, while restraining them from coagulating so as to form anything as monumental as they have become.

The fact is that Papanoutsos does and does not accept realism, and does and does not accept idealism—and this not because of philosophical indecision, but because of his thoroughly controlled way of looking at them. Consider idealism first. Note was taken at the end of the last section of his insistence that the intellectual level at which idealism emerges, where the syntax of "reality" is the very stuff of mind or intellect, is no philosophical phantasm, but is in fact reached in various modern scientific theorizings. The spirit of these is indeed idealist; reality can indeed present itself (or be presented) in an idealist aspect. But in conceding this much, there is a danger of erroneous extrapolation. The theoretical habit of mind can become, as it were, imperialistic. The modern mathematically structured sciences are, it may be suggested, both the crowning achievement of and the proper model for the human intellect in its dealings with "reality." If anyone has accentuated the venerable distinction between appearances and reality by showing us the astonishing picture of mathematical "reality," it is the modern mathematical physicist. His categories, idealist categories, then, might seem to be those which most appropriately comprehend the "real" nature of things. While open to revision, they are liable to no sort of "reification"—

not now, now that we have come so far in the direction of "intellectualization."

This is hard-line idealism. According to Papanoutsos it is a "dogma,"[13] and as such unacceptable. Its proponents, he suggests, have arrived at it because of the following beliefs, which he rejects: first, "that only theoretical reason has the right to be heard in solving the ontological problem [matter of perplexity, *aporia*]"; and second, "that being will be given its correct significance only when investigated from the point of view of pure thought."[14] What appears to be at issue here is two principles: one that we deal with "the world" practically as well as theoretically, and that our practical transactions are with something that is every bit as "real" in terms of those transactions as is "the world" represented as the object of mathematical physics: the other that there is, after all, perception as well as pure thought, and that what perception delivers to us is not *negatived* because of the successes of what pure thought achieves in its own terms. It may be suggested that the style of these principles is extremely relative. Probably Papanoutsos would agree, and would not see the relativity as being a blemish.

Let us turn now to realism. The intellectual level at which realism emerges is partly that of common sense, partly that of the patient, positive, "fact"-collecting and "fact"-classifying sciences of which Bacon and Mill were possibly the best-known theorists. Here again we are dealing with a genuine dimension of mind, a context in which the realist spirit is perfectly appropriate. But here also there is a temptation to extrapolate, and to move to a dogmatic realism which for Papanoutsos is just as unacceptable as dogmatic idealism. Hard-line realism, he complains, "regards consciousness at all its levels as an appendage of being."[15] The notorious ambiguity of "being" shows up in this pronouncement. Papanoutsos's point is better put when he complains of the exclusiveness of the model (that of perception) which is held by realism to be the paradigm of "dependable" knowledge. Knowledge is explained as "a mode . . . in which one being is 'represented' in another which awaits the determinations of the first and receives them obediently."[16] But, as we have seen, the intellect does have a *penetrative* power; and also, practical activity, which was resistant to the claims of hard-line idealism in one way, is resistant in another way to those of hard-line realism. Papanoutsos's thinking on this last point is enigmatic to a degree. It may be that in some way the initiatives which we can take "against" nature, and the free choices and decisions of which, in certain circumstances, we are capable, cast doubt on the picture of *cognitive* determination and submission which hard-line realism presents; but if this is so, the connection is left obscure. This consideration, fortunately, does not vitiate the rest of Papanoutsos's argument on the present subject matter.

The general position which Papanoutsos has now reached in regard to realism and idealism is one to which attention was drawn in outlining the two forms of "positive" dialectical relationship which Papanoutsos presented schematically in his section on "Forms of Dialectic."[17] Briefly, realism and idealism are not antithetic, are propounded not from the same point of view but from two different ones, and are complementary. In the language of that section, they stand in a "closed" form of dialectical relationship. The discovery of this is a "solution" of the problem which they present.

Resolution of the Problem.[18] Realism and idealism, it has been argued, are comprehensible points of view when each is confined to an appropriate style of enquiry. And they are complementary. What does their "complementarity" mean? It could mean that there is no going beyond either of them. We adopt one or the other point of view according to the way in which we play out the "investigations" which we undertake into the ultimate character of our problematic universe. The one may supply what the other lacks, but there can be no overall view of that universe except what is provided by the external, side-by-side conjunction of the two. This would be a "synthesis" of the most rudimentary sort, a putting of the two together without any qualification of the one by the other; with no prospect of our adopting a third position to which each in its way contributes. Now, is this wrong? Can their complementarity yield a view of the world which is "beyond" each of them? Can we reach a synthesis which owes something to each of them, but which is also a recognizably new position?

Papanoutsos has made so much of the relativity of the two points of view that it might seem difficult for him to accept the possibility of a synthesis of the second, more progressive, kind. And yet, it would also seem, this is what he must try to do if confidence in the dialectical method as a fertile method of enquiry is to be justified. And indeed, toward the end of Papanoutsos's discussion of the ontological problem the reader becomes aware of a change of emphasis. The patient analysis has been accomplished: we see where and to what extent realism is at home, and we locate idealism correspondingly. But now dissatisfaction returns. Neither, really (Papanoutsos is now allowing us to suspect), is a position that is *sufficient* even at the level at which it naturally suggests itself. Having, as it were, seen through them, the critical philosopher may come to realize that each lacks the other in the sense, not just of making no provision for the other, but of painfully requiring the other for the rounding out of a coherent philosophical point of view. Does this idea work out?

Realism, it would appear, remains insistent that it should be heard, after all the analyzing is over. Papanoutsos thinks that at the end of his discussion he is in a position to say the following, meager in a way though it is:

Reality is something *positive* endowed with an inner *dynamism,* a power which asserts itself in a context of struggle, i.e. in resistance to its own suppression. This feature is vouchsafed to us *directly* (in the exercise of our voluntary activity) and it comes into conflict with the standpoint of idealism. . . .[19]

Papanoutsos seems to be allowing realism and idealism to fight it out, just when he has contrived to put each of them in its proper place! Can idealism also, then, reassert itself ? Papanoutsos also says:

Reality is a *multiplicity* which does not preclude *variety.* This feature we deduce indirectly from the number and variety of the methods used by theoretical consciousness in order to grasp and interpret it.[20]

This looks like a compensating concession to idealism. But it is not at all clear that it is, for Papanoutsos at once confesses that the number and variety of its interpretative means, like the number and variety of our modes of perception is an embarrassment to idealism. The situation may be *either* (as apparently suggested above) that reality is like what this state of inhomogeneity indicates, *or* that we are hopelessly at odds with reality, which is unitary in a way that our schemes of thought cannot grasp. The two passages quoted are introduced as if they represent, summarily, the most that critical philosophy can say in answer to the question, "What is the essence of *being?*" The first is proposed confidently enough, but the second, no sooner than propounded, is hedged about with doubts and qualifications which, in effect, annul it. Is there no redemption left for idealism, therefore, corresponding to that which is conceded to realism in the first of the passages quoted?

Yes, there is an enigmatic redemption, to be glimpsed a little earlier than the passages, quoted above, which are causing the difficulty. Papanoutsos does think that there can be a dialectical synthesis of realism and idealism, in their partiality, into "a unified, integrated view of things."[21] Cryptically, he says that "the subject gains in self-awareness through the object, the object in reality through the subject."[22] How can the object "gain in reality" through the subject? If it can do this, then the idealist emphasis, it would seem, can be revived without repelling, as it were, the realist one. It is a question, Papanoutsos suggests, of recognizing the validity of the concept or concepts which from the theoretical scientific point of view *are* the very substance of the "object" which we are striving to know.[23] The object becomes "more real" inasmuch as, through conceptualization, more account can be taken of it in more different ways.

Here we have a return to the old idealist preoccupation with "degrees of reality"; and so long as the explanation of what is involved is careful enough, no harm is done by reviving it. But for present purposes the point which is involved is this: that whereas hitherto—in bringing out the "three concepts" of subjectivity (and of objectivity)—we recorded the realist and the idealist emphases separately and independently and with the minimum of regard for one another, that is not how we should leave the position in the end of the day. Without sacrificing the clarity we have gained, but, rather, taking advantage of it, we can now achieve a comprehensive view of the subject-object relationship in which realism and idealism emerge in a certain tension with one another, but only as putting a demand on one another that each recognize the very fact that it provides a context for the other. It is best to put this final "solution" in Papanoutsos's own terms, which make it clear that the complementarity with which he credits realism and idealism is of an integrated type, and not simply the juxtaposition of two standpoints of which the possibility was mooted at the beginning of this section. They also make it clear that in this whole discussion the dialectical process, difficult as the terrain has been at many points, has not stopped short of its full objective as it seemed in danger, at one stage, of doing.

The law governing the situation confronting us can accurately be expressed in terms of a bilateral reference, a dialectical interdependence. The consciousness of the ego and certainty of the self-existence of being as nonego are established by the same procedure, confirmed and steadily renewed by it. The conditions governing consciousness and being in all their peculiarities and contrasts are formed for perception and thought upon the same foundations, with the same force and with the same necessity (on the practical level first of all and then on the theoretical). Self-consciousness not only does not come into conflict with the acknowledgment of a stubbornly independent reality, but actually confirms such acknowledgment, just as it itself is confirmed by the affirmation of that reality. We have to do here with independent but nevertheless correlated forces: through their correlation their independence, far from being subverted, is actually made more explicit.[24]

In the hope that the reader can see light in this tough but characteristic passage, the author will leave Papanoutsos's ontological problem there. If the reader cannot see light, this will not be for want of preparatory effort on Papanoutsos's part. The dialectical method is not unthorough, but it *is* unrigid. And its (deliberate) unrigidity may bring difficulties in train. There is no question of a formal, mechanical treatment of a problem, of a stereotyped negation of antithetic positions yielding some formal, transendent "synthesis" which represents the solution of whatever is in question, and which, because of its very formality, may be superficially easy to grasp. Papanoutsos does not use this sort of apparatus. If "negation" comes into the procedure, the degree to which one "-ism," over against another, has to be negated may vary enormously from problem to problem, and sometimes the idea of "negation"—as distinct, for example, from "supplementation" (leading perhaps to "complementarity")— may not even be particularly apropos. Such has been the case in the discussion just reviewed. As a result it may be that—as here—the considered answer to a problem is bulky and difficult to make compendious (although apophthegms are far from being absent from Papanoutsos's work). But at least, it can be claimed, a real attempt has been made to do justice to the problem in the round.

The Gnosiological Problem

The Meaning of "Gnosiology." Gnosiology is obviously a theory of *gnosis,* but how are we to understand *gnosis?* This term appears crucially in Plato's *Republic,* signifying generally "knowledge of Being or Truth, i.e. the Ideas," in Adam's phrase.[25] With belief and ignorance, *gnosis* makes up that set of prospects which exists for the human mind in its enquiring relationship to the world in which it finds itself. Characteristically, the term is associated with clarity about whatever it is that the mind has to do with. Belief, it is said, is "darker than *gnosis,* and brighter than ignorance."[26] The clarity in which *gnosis* excels belief may be explained in other terms as the articulation (where articulation there is) of what is known, an articulation "seen" as a feature either of that "thing" in itself or of that "thing" in its context. Whether the "seeing" is more of an immediate intuition or more an achievment of reasoning is problematic; but at least we can say that in *gnosis* the mind is face to face with what is authentic or original as distinct from what is secondary or derived. A theory of *gnosis* would certainly be a theory about the *foundations* of what is known, and Papanoutsos's "gnosiology" is thus far on Platonic lines.

In his book called *Gnosiology*, however, Papanoutsos himself says curiously little about the lineage of this term or about the definitional significance which it has for him. "Gnosiology" is an unfamiliar term in English-language philosophy. What differentiates gnosiology from epistemology? Epistemology is a discipline well-enough known, but it represents "theory of knowledge" in some way that differs, in scope or in method of treatment, from that in which Papanoutsos's "gnosiology" represents it. Papanoutsos appears to regard "gnosiology" as the more comprehensive term of the two, and in this respect he is not obviously working on Platonic lines.[27]

It may seem as if an attempt to formulate a succint definitional distinction between the two terms is an instance of misplaced pedantic optimism; but help comes from an unexpected quarter. The distinction is recognized, it happens, in Italian philosophy, and it can be found in a lexicographical form which seems to correspond to Papanoutsos's philosophical intentions. Epistemology, it has been proposed, is that "part of philosophy which interests itself in the sciences, and studies in particular their principles and methods, so as to assess their validity on the logical level."[28] This definition, with its concentration on "the sciences," looks relatively narrow; its emphasis is on theory construction; it is "extensional" in that it has reference to the works, rather than the workings, of the mind which engages in the sciences. Now compare the definition of "gnosiology": gnosiology is the "study of cognition *(conoscenza)*, that is of the possibility, validity and limits of human cognitive activity."[29] However we choose to explain "cognition," this definition does envisage a study of the powers of the mind which is not confined to one rather special sector of the mind's activities, namely theory construction. And it does contain in embryo the great scheme which Papanoutsos's study undertakes. For consider what is involved in the following, the main subject matter of his *Gnosiology*: being and consciousness; experience and reason; common sense and science; nature and history; philosophy and religion. However much an English-

speaking philosopher's definition of "epistemology" might con-
flate the two Italian definitions of "epistemology" and "gnosiology" given above, and draw into itself "gnosiological" elements,[30]
it is clear that epistemology would still fall short, in its ambitions,
of envisaging a program like that of Papanoutsos, into which
much else, including problems of metaphysics and philosophy
of mind, conspicuously enters.

It is not inappropriate to compare Papanoutsos's subject matter,
in point of scope, with certain seventeenth- or eighteenth-century
examples; for instance, in the explanation of that subject matter,
the scope of Locke's or Hume's "understanding" or of Reid's
"intellectual powers"; and to construe the title of his book in
some such fashion as "Theory of the Intellectual Powers." Thus,
indeed, is more than just a minor matter of terminology. The
meaning which is to be put on "gnosiology," and the practice
of gnosiology as displayed in Papanoutsos's book, are connected
with an important philosophical ideal—that philosophical thinking should strive to remain capable of surveying and assessing,
after its fashion, whatever systems of ideas human beings may
construct either to interpret or to alter their world. The demands
on philosophical *comprehension* (in more than one sense of the term)
become continuously greater; and yet, whatever be the difficulties
in satisfying the ideal of comprehension, it is also an ideal (partly
a moral one, perhaps) that philosophers as a class should not
admit defeat in face of them. In particular, they should not fence
off the subject (as English-speaking philosophers were tending
to do a generation ago) so as to confine it to an examination of
"systems" regarded purely for their interest as logical constructions; nor should they resign themselves to thinking of "truth"
as being radically heterogeneous, a collection of ways of thinking
of which we can but say that "they serve."

The Dialogue of Experience and Reason.[31] The scope and
variety of the topics which will now be discussed in this section
should help to indicate further the difference between "gnosiology," as Papanoutsos understands it, and "epistemology." The
discussion of epistemological problems in the next chapter will,
it is to be hoped, also contribute to this end.

From the ontological problem couched in terms of realism versus idealism, Papanoutsos moves to the associated methodological one, as he calls it, of empiricism versus rationalism. Here, correspondingly, his technique is to show where, in the general setting of human capacities, needs and experiences, the one and the other of those two traditionally "antithetic" points of view are at home, or most at home. The question that prompts this Janus-faced solution can be put in two ways: (1) If you take the interdependent forms of thought and modes of working which make up our rationality—disciplined, self-conscious, and purposive as it is—to what is all this due? To the pressure of things to which it is subjected via the senses, or to a free productive capacity of the mind's own? (2) The world of knowledge is fashioned from experience but also from thought. Experience presents us with a world that is varied and in process, whereas the mind proffers unity and stability. How can these apparently irreconcilable offerings—of otherness and identity—come together?

It can be suggested that Papanoutsos's answer to questions of this style is essentially Kantian, being his own version of the dictum that "thoughts without content are empty, intuitions without concepts are blind."[32] His version is basically the simple consideration that experience and reason cannot leave one another alone. Papanoutsos explains:

The a posteriori data [with which we are concerned in any systematic scientific or philosphical research] make possible the a priori method which will process them; Experience *poses* the questions and Reason provides the *solution*. (We are all aware to what extent the posing of a question, without constituting a solution, makes one possible and after that manner contains it.)[33]

It has to be confessed that the thought, thus developed, no longer seems so simple; but it is fair to add that the author has reached this passage by cutting a long, dialectical argument short. And of course, as Papanoutsos well recognizes, there are situations in which experience and reason are only too happy to leave one another alone. But he is not much interested in the crude particularity, on the one hand, and the formal sterilities, on the other, which result when this inclination is granted.

How in fact *are* experience and reason related dialectically, in his view? Toward the end of his discussion of their relationship, Papanoutsos puts the position summarily, in the following fashion:

(1) That scientific knowledge is *not* just a matter of assembling and classifying material yielded by observation; instead, such material is to be organized within a rational framework of concepts and explanatory principles; *but* this latter activity requires constant reference to, and submission to check by, experience.

(2) More sophisticatedly: that in the experimental sciences the so-called "data" recorded by observation do not come at us, so to speak, as pure and original items, but are selected, after a fashion prepared, and in important ways modified according to the style of scientific thinking by which they are being studied, and the way in which, in that style of thought, heuristic or probative experiments, as the case may be, are organized. It is well to remember that an experiment is an answer to a question, and that "Nature rarely reveals her secrets spontaneously."[34]

(3) That even in mathematics there is nothing which can be likened to parthenogenesis. Experience, as well as providing areas of application for mathematical thought, is what fertilizes mathematical thought in the first place. And even here experience and reason cannot leave one another alone. Mathematics *is* applicable—or is always to be held potentially applicable—to nonmathematical reality. And nonmathematical reality *is* mathematizable—or is always to be held potentially such.

Comment will not be offered here on the controversial aspects of point (3) since Papanoutsos's discussions of mathematics will be reviewed at a later stage. What needs to be brought out, however, is the nature of the *dialectical* connection between reason and experience summarized as above. Reason does not reflect experience passively; it does not receive its *schemes of things* from experience. On the other hand it is not related to experience in a sheerly a priori manner; it does not absolutely dictate to experience. The relationship of reason and experience is the history of an "endless interchange of actions and reactions."[35] Reason struggles to cast an ever finer and more sophisticated—and at the same time broader and more unified—system of nets over what experience confronts or can be made to confront it with. But it is the very resistance, the difficulties and problems presented by experience, which keeps this dynamic process in operation. "The pattern of this struggle . . . will always be one of alternation: experience will keep on attempting to flood consciousness with the wealth and variety of its data, and reason will persist in an effort to order this multiplicity by means of the most stable and the most clearly articulated discipline which thought can attain."[36]

Papanoutsos is returning here to the theme of dynamic alternation to which, in his discussion of the forms of dialectic, he awards the palm.[37] In homely terms, reason and experience do not settle for complementarity. They keep going at one another. Papanoutsos more than once contrasts the dynamic style of thought, of which he writes approvingly, with "static," of which he is severely critical. And he takes the opportunity, presented by his discussion of experience and reason, to be critical, in this way, even of some "evolutionary" thinking. Static theories do their utmost to eliminate from their reckoning such factors as "productive movement, essential differentiation, stages and gradations, maintenance of antitheses, interdependence of conflicting conditions, and the like."[38] (This is not the place in which to attempt the difficult task of spelling out the meaning of these phrases.) Instead they aim at "reduction"; in general terms, of the later to the earlier, of the near at hand to the far off, of the complex to the less complex, of the advanced to the elementary, and so on. The ideal of such reductions is simplification. What they achieve, Papanoutsos thinks, is often oversimplification— a slashing at problems instead of a solution to them. And, that a theory may base itself on the notion of development or evolution is no guarantee that it is of a dynamic rather than a static character. If the solution, viewed as it were from finish to start, is reductive, the theory concerned is suspect.

For example, an evolutionary theory which maintained that all the great features of reality that creation has yielded, from the elementary particle of physics, the electron, to the most delicate flowering of life which is human thought, can be placed on the same level, put on the same line of progression, treated as phases of one and the same working-out of things, in the sense that the same laws can render an account of all the successive moments in this long-drawn-out series of events, would certainly be a static theory. Its mode of explanation, negating inhomogeneity and treating as alike what is not alike, repudiates the essential concept of productiveness, of creative force as an organic factor in cosmic development, and thus transforms *evolution* into a static notion.[39]

This vigorous declaration exhibits both Papanoutsos's pluralism and, in an oblique way, his humanism. But the latter is a topic which will have to be treated on its own at a later stage.

Analysis and Synthesis.[40] Papanoutsos draws attention, in various ways, to the "alternating" rhythm of our advances in knowledge. One example of alternation is the way in which our mind addresses itself to its subject matter with a perspective which switches from the analytical to the synthetic, and the synthetic to the analytical, on a succession of levels which it may occupy in the process of broadening and deepening what we claim to know. This process, once more, is to be construed dialectically. Papanoutsos notes, interestingly, that we may reach a certain stage in it when we feel justified in applying to our results the honorific label, "truth." The question just how a dialectical alternation can reach such a position of equilibrium that this degree of finality (and of confidence) can be reached, will be worth examining.

"Analysis" in this context means a disjoining of the elements of some perceptual or conceptual whole *(Gestalt)*, and "synthesis" their reassembly in a new logical unity. The one process followed by the other allows us to apprehend them as having a different structure from before; they present themselves to us in a new interrelationship; and this furthers our understanding of whatever it is we began with. Now this process is dynamic, and repeated. Why? The answer, in simple terms, is that seeing some complex of things in a new light is suggestive—of analogies, of the possibility of extending this complex so as to comprehend classes of items that have not hitherto been covered by the conceptual structure or structures with which we have been working. But will the existing structure or structures do? Probably not. In order to give coverage to so much new material we are going to need not a stretched but a rearticulated and more powerful theoretical apparatus. And by working this out we shall move one stage further up the scale of comprehension of our "universe of discourse," whatever it is. But then, any success which we thus achieve on the side of theory construction will have its repercussions in the opening up of new analytical prospects. Can we disengage new elements from some new, not hitherto worked, field of enquiry which our theory might possibly cover?—and so on.

Two demands, as Papanoutsos calls them, impel us in advancing along these lines: the one is for "greater objectivity" (i.e., greater objective rapport and coverage), and the other for "more perfect organization" (i.e., a tauter as well as more complete theoretical scheme).[41] These two demands stand in a dialectical relationship. It is difficult (to say the least) to satisfy the one while concentrating on the other. But at the same time each gives rise to the other. The more you try to explain by means of it, the better you want your theory to be: and the better your theory, the more you want to try to explain by means of it.

An enlightening synthesis, based upon a penetrating analysis, will tend naturally to result in a period of "equilibrium."[42] This is to be understood not as a period in which the mind stops thinking about whatever it has been concerned with, but rather as one in which the mind becomes "at home," both with its new theoretical scheme and with the extended range of application which is that scheme's counterpart. In this context, however, "equilibrium" must be a relative matter. For part of the very process of intellectual adjustment is testing. One has to try to see what fits into the new scheme of things and what does not: also, one has to try to see how precisely the new scheme applies to and explains various kinds of item that have now become its business. So that there is no guarantee how stable any period of relative equilibrium will be, how long we shall be disposed to go on allowing that this *is* a period of relative equilibrium.

Papanoutsos himself insists, again and again, that no intellectual achievement can afford to be so confident of itself as to exempt itself from a future of trial and testing. Indeed he writes at times as if it were a *moral* obligation upon the scientist or other kind of theorist to recognize the permanent relevance of doubt vis-à-vis the theory which he sponsors, or, to put it a little less strongly, to acknowledge the virtue of constant open-mindedness in regard to it.[43] Hence it is strange to find him remarking that the achievement of equilibrium—following how great a succession of analyses and syntheses he does not say—can be identified with that of truth. After an outline account of what "equilibrium," understood in terms of his "two demands" described above, comprises, he intersperses the observation that "this equilibrium we denominate: *truth.*"[44] The word "intersperses" is appropriate because he does not pursue the theme of "truth" at this juncture. Instead, the emphasis of what follows is on how recurrent are the "two demands" and how *destructive* is their effect upon equilibrium once achieved.

It is not clear who are the "we" who denominate equilibrium, at a certain stage, *truth.* If Papanoutsos is simply remarking that that is what people (perhaps nontheorists) naturally tend or are tempted to do, then with this sociological observation one can have little quarrel. If, however, he is lending some assent to their mode of usage, it is difficult to reconcile this with his general dialectical standpoint. He is no pragmatist, such as to have patience with the slogan that truth is what serves. His own outlook would seem to require that he rather regard *truth* as an "ideal of reason" in the Kantian sense, a supreme value which, so far as knowledge of our world is concerned, we know how to recognize and adopt as our guide, but which we shall not expect, ever, to see face to face. Papanoutsos's more considered views about truth, however, will be discussed in a subsequent subsection of this chapter.

Gradations of Knowledge.[45]   In the last subsection an attempt was made to describe, in very general terms such as Pa-

panoutsos himself uses, how the field of knowledge as a whole
is determined at any given time by the pervasive, but alternating,
human activities of analysis and synthesis. This same field of
knowledge, however, can be reviewed in terms of what Papanoutsos calls "gradations,"[46] a series of progressions from the
simplest and most spontaneous grasp of things to the most complex and comprehensive. Such a review is his next undertaking.
Here the dialectical character of the relationship between one
phase of knowledge, as he discusses it, and another, is less apparent than elsewhere; but it does show itself once or twice, and
in any case the reader (Papanoutsos must hope) should now be
in a position to assign it its *implicit* importance. It is to be noted
also at the outset that in describing "gradations" of knowledge,
Papanoutsos is not writing in historical terms. Neither human
knowledge as a whole, nor the knowledge of any particular individual, has developed or develops according to the neatly
marked-out progression which Papanoutsos now sketches for us.
Human knowledge as a whole may manifest any of the "gradations" described, at particular points of the great patchwork that
it is; or it may be a complex of them; and any individual may
be involved with more than one gradation in this or that situation.
Summarily, what we have to do with is not strict historical phases
in the advance of knowledge, but *given* aspects of knowledge
ordered in terms of sophistication and comprehension—or, of the
mind's articulate dominance over its different kinds of subject
matter.

   We begin with the *perceptual* level. Phenomenologically, this
is where we must begin, for Papanoutsos regards sensations, as
distinct from perceptions, not as entities, but only as abstractly
isolable features of perceptions. A perception is an encounter with
reality, optically, acoustically, and so on: an elementary *experience*
of it, with all that that involves *more than* the occurrence of a
mere sensation. The phrase "impressions of perception" is familiar
enough in philosophy, and Papanoutsos himself uses it here. But
the word "impression" is ambiguous: it may convey the idea of
something stamped or impressed on us, we being wholly passive
terms in this relationship; or it may be allowed to suggest a

particular way in which we are "impressed by" reality, as if the direction which our perceptual experience takes, and the quality characteristic of it in various settings, were not altogether independent of our interests, intentions, and desires (in a word borrowed from Sartre, our "projects"). It is probably in the second of these ways that Papanoutsos means his "impressions" of perception to be taken, and this may be part of what is involved in his insistence on maintaining a distinction between perception and sensation. But he does not, in the present context, make the point explicit.

What he does highlight is the nature of a perceptual "representation," namely, that which is retained by us of a perceptual impression, as bearing upon more or less immediately consequent experience. The "representation" of something, thus remaining with us, is importantly selective; knowingly or not, we emphasize some features of that "thing," and play down or expunge others, according to interest, disposition, or need. A rudimentary, most rudimentary, "organization" is involved in the process. Yet, for all that it does not go deep, such organization, as Papanoutsos remarks intriguingly, "represents a degree of morphological accomplishment [*aretē*]" through which "the representation acquires significance and can *symbolize* something."[47]

This accomplishment, though, *is* very defective in the way in which it meets the second of Papanoutsos's two demands, for objectification and for organization, described (with a dialectical reference) in the last section. Perceptual representations crowd in on us; they contrive to group themselves and be classified after a fashion, but this is associative and not logical, and so cannot comprise an "articulated" view, on our part, of the objective world which, in perception, we confront. To get articulation, we need concept formation. This activity is the work of "a more demanding, creative consciousness"[48] than is the elementary capacity to perceive. There are many varieties of concept, and Papanoutsos gives numerous examples of these: simple and complex, definite and indefinite, theoretic and practical, and so on. Whereas the establishment of "representations" was simply a first move in the direction of *meaningful* thinking, that of concepts, whatever their variety, is in effect the installation, into thinking, of logic. Concepts are selections and abstractions of features perceived of our world and as such susceptible of logical interrelationship. (Papanoutsos is not considering in this context logical concepts themselves—at any rate not directly. His concern is with a basis of comparison between the representational and the conceptual, and this limits his terms of reference accordingly.) To put it colloquially: in the perceptual we are liable to get bogged down; the conceptual assists us to free ourselves.

The representation in all its perceptual fullness has a restricted significance from a theoretical point of view. For this very fullness confines and binds the mind to the "material" factor in experience, while the concept liberates it, and opens the way to more daring intellectual constructions.[49]

Among these more daring intellectual constructions Papanoutsos includes "principles and laws, hypotheses and theories, descriptions and interpretations, diagrams and arguments."[50] He applies to such items the Platonic term "ideas." Although "theories" enter into his list, he seems to have in mind here intellectual devices and activities which fall short of being systems proper. These items are presented as what the mind does with its concepts in the first instance. It has these ways of combining and deploying its concepts in the interests of methodological effectiveness. They represent a step forward on the side of organization, as if the mind were assembling and reviewing its resources as a propaedeutic to more single-minded theoretical enterprises, namely the special sciences. "Theories" would seem to be interpretable, in this context, only as relatively tentative constructions; bits of theorizing about this or that, perhaps.

So we come to Papanoutsos's fourth gradation, "systems of ideas" taking form as the special sciences, physical, social, or of another kind. (Papanoutsos in fact recognizes an unconventionally wide variety of "special sciences," including in this category not only, for example, Physics, Chemistry, Geology, Biology, Psychology, and Sociology, but also History, Law, and Philology. It would not be appropriate here to enter into a dispute about demarcation.)[51] These sciences are "special" because of the relatively well-defined and clearly delimited nature of their subject matter, each claiming a field for investigation and elucidation to which, in a well-organized and disciplinary fashion, it directs itself expressly. (Not that there cannot be boundary disputes among the special sciences or, beneficially, boundary extensions or overlapping; but that is another matter.) The formation of the special sciences does represent an advance, in theory construction, on anything available in the preceding grade of knowledge. But at least as conspicuous an advance is the reinforcement and extension of "objectivity" which a special science achieves. By setting itself to "capture," methodically as it does, whatever may have a claim to homogeneity with its already-established concerns, a special science both confirms and broadens the scope of its involvement with the world. It exposes itself to further test, while also maintaining, so far as it fairly can, the style and the authority which it has come to exercise in the interpretation of its objects hitherto.

Papanoutsos's fifth gradation is one of which he speaks only briefly and conditionally. It "would be"—the phrase is his—a "system of systems."[52] The ultimate possibility of a unified science, usually envisaged as a form of physics, is a familiar enough topic in modern philosophy of science. Papanoutsos, however, appears to be envisaging something even wider. He sketches his idea, or ideal, of a system of systems in terms of ideally extended intercommunication, made possible by a common "scientific" language consisting of both a common verbal symbolism and a common syntax. By means of such a language we should be able to achieve clear and adequate communication of "physicist and chemist with geologist and biologist, of the four with psychologist and sociologist, and of all of these together with anthropologist and theologian," and end product being a "general and comprehensive theory of the world and of life."[53] Suffice it to remark that this ideal *can* have a beneficial effect on our intellectual progress.

In Papanoutsos's discussion of the gradations of knowledge there is little or no mention of either mathematics or philosophy.

He discusses each of these elsewhere, but clearly they ought to come into the present reckoning somehow. Mathematics, it may be suggested, does so as a cardinal feature of the organization of scientific thought in coming to terms with its world. It therefore has an implicit but easily assignable place in the fourth "gradation." Of philosophy Papanoutsos says, almost wistfully, that it used to have to bear the expectations of those who regarded a system of systems as in some way realizable. As it is, he does not assign it to a particular gradation. Perhaps it should have one of its own, somewhere between the fourth and the fifth.

The Perceptual Spectrum.   The differentiation of perception from sensation is a theme to which Papanoutsos returns in *Reason and Man*.[54] He does so partly in order to confirm his view that mere sensation does not occur on its own, but that sensation, in real experience, is embedded in perception; and to explain what this means. More interestingly, perhaps, he uses the relationship between the two, as he sees it, as a cue to the relationship between perception and a wider cognitive context. Just how isolable is an act of perceiving?

Let us return, then, to "sensation." The notion of a sense datum, the identification of sense data, and the recognition which these may be due as items in our experience, together have constituted a bone of contention in much fairly recent philosophical argument. Should we not be prepared to recognize that there are simple or immediate impressions of sense: for example, the registering of a blue color as distinct from a blue sky, of a feeling of rocking as distinct from the rocking of one's body, or of pain as distinct from a sore head or tooth? No, answers Papanoutsos, noting in this regard, but not drawing on, the support of *Gestalt* and other recent psychology. These "simples" or "immediate" items which we are said to "register" belong not to the concrete world of natural experience, but to an abstract, artificial one— a philosophers' contrivance. We do not stop short, he seems to say, of *something like* seeing a blue sky, feeling our body rock, having a sore head, and so on. To achieve the so-called "immediacy" of seeing blue, of rocking, or of soreness we have to work at it! Papanoutsos concedes that certain psychological experiments (which he does not specify) *may* come near to achieving (in a manner of speaking) sensations of color, sound, or odor as distinct from full-blooded seeing, hearing, and smelling. They do so by attempting to suspend whatever development upon color, sound, or odor makes up, naturally and normally, ordinary experience "of" these things. But he is doubtful whether the suspension is entire; and, in any case, the very difficulty of these experiments is the exception that proves the rule. Experience of the physical world then, if he is right, is never *less than* perceptual. But what "perceptual" experience itself involves has yet to be elucidated.

This topic is introduced by means of three examples. We do speak, for instance, of "perceiving" a ripe apple. We may claim to have a "perception" of depth, say in a collage. And we may claim to "perceive" where a certain sound is coming from. But now, granted all that has been said about the distinction between sensation and perception, perception is *sense* perception. And to what *sense* can we ascribe our awareness of the ripeness of the apple, the depth of the collage, or the direction of the sound? None. Nor is there any question of the senses contributing to this awareness in some kind of concert with one another.

It would be too much, however, to suggest that some process of reasoning is involved. When we "perceive" a ripe apple we do not *argue,* from premises more or less explicit, to a conclusion that this apple is ripe. It is not a matter of bringing past experience to bear calculatingly, of taking an inductive attitude toward this apple because other apples which have looked like that have turned out to be ripe. The perceptions of the senses are perhaps not the whole story, but in this as in the other two examples mentioned we are, Papanoutsos insists, experiencing something as immediately as ever it can be experienced. And to this there is no genetic build-up from the nonimmediate, from a mental process. Right from the outset, Papanoutsos is willing to risk saying, consciousness can inform us of something's ripeness, depth, direction and so on, immediately, without discursive reasoning.[55]

This may seem a strange and perhaps unwarranted point of view. How can the ripeness of an apple be conveyed to us immediately except as a kind of unthinking bonus of habit and custom? We have first to learn how to recognize ripeness. The ability to do so may be treated as an accomplishment, the exercise of which can indeed take place "immediately." But the learning itself must certainly involve processes of reasoning. In addition, our "recognition" of an apple's ripeness may be uncertain and tentative. We may doubt, for reasons such as that the apple simply looks too green, whether the apple is ripe. Quite often we do not take in its ripeness at a glance! When we do, are we not presupposing the "ratiocinative" background of which Papanoutsos would have us innocent? As Hume might have relished pointing out, to be able to recognize ripeness in an apple we do need a background of previous cognitive experience, more or less attentive, every bit as much as Adam (in the Garden of Eden) would have needed such experience before he could tell what would happen if the divine provider had furnished him with a billiard table, billiard balls, and a cue, and he himself had the curiosity to propel one billiard ball in the direction of another.

Could Papanoutsos reply in some such fashion as the following? "I am talking not about learning to recognize ripeness, but about recognizing it. The former may well involve discursive reasoning; the latter does not. Nor am I talking about a state of uncertainty as to the ripeness of a piece of fruit. In our uncertainty we may well employ discursive reasoning in order to resolve the uncertainty in one way or the other. I am talking about the phenomenologically indubitable 'perception' of a piece of fruit as being ripe. What enters into this experience is sight or smell or taste, memory perhaps as conveying familiarity, and recognition by the mind of what these features *signify*. What is loosely called 'perception' here is, in fact, a very complex experience, involving not only perception in a narrower sense, but other 'powers of the mind' which are integrated with it. What is not involved is any kind of logical argumentation, undertaken by the mind in soliloquy with itself."

It seems reasonable to suggest that some such reply is implicit in Papanoutsos's difficult discussion of the present problem. The author is not convinced that, granted a certain "immediacy" in the experiences which have been taken as examples for discussion, the lineage of such experiences does not include discursive reasoning. On the contrary, it seems probable that it does—although the reasoning need not have been of a sophisticated sort—and that Papanoutsos is incautious in challenging *to this extent*—as he does—that school of rational psychology which would have reasoning be a feature of the most "immediate"-looking experiences such as he selects for discussion. The reader may feel, perhaps, that this subject matter is more of psychological than of philosophical interest. Papanoutsos would probably concede— or for that matter claim—that the subject matter is borderline. Be that as it may. The particular kind of interest which his discussion presents is one thing; his overall motive for undertaking this discussion, another, which he has broached elsewhere in a variety of ways. His attitude to the compartmentalization of human cognitive activity (of which the old "faculty" psychology was indeed a particular example, in one possible style of theorizing about this subject) is constantly critical. To make *sense* of our sense perception more is involved than just sense perception. How far we may want to go in delineating a context within which we may say that this or that perceptual experience makes sense is to some extent, as the discussion in the present section may have suggested, controversial. But this does not affect Papanoutsos's insistence on the essential integration of the mind's activities. (No "logical empiricist" is he.) It is a paradoxical feature of his account, all the same, that while our awareness of the ripeness of an apple, for example, is an "immediate" experience,[56] the perceptual impressions on which that awareness is based have to be "mediated,"[57] through memory and—dare one use the term?—apperception, to constitute a significant whole.

Concepts under Transformation. In a preceding subsection an account was given of how Papanoutsos sees the significance of concept formation as being both the primary logical articulation of thought and the liberation of thought from entanglement in the particular. Sense perception may be said to dictate the need for concepts, but it does not in all respects dictate what concepts the mind actually forms. In forming concepts the mind functions creatively. Its introduction of logic into the situation is creative, as also is its ability to envisage and entertain alternative concepts in relation to some specific perceptual or other manifold. Obviously, an important feature of this way of looking at concepts is a sensitiveness to their liability to change. Our conceptual equipment is open at any time to modification. Some concepts we shall be prepared to abandon, others we shall introduce as new, and others we shall qualify or transform in this way or that. There may be occasions, however, when we cannot do any one of these things definitively and to our satisfaction. There may be occasions when we have to operate with certain existing concepts *faute de mieux,* to go on using old ones on sufferance pending the formation of something new and more adequate. We may even find ourselves in this position when attempting in certain circumstances to make use of concepts that are very general and deeply entrenched.

This is the subject to which Papanoutsos devotes himself in an essay called "Concepts under Transformation."[58] His general preference for depicting the human intellect as dynamic rather than contemplative is again apparent in this piece. Also, the essay illustrates a particular dialectical fork on which the intellect may be caught, although Papanoutsos is again allowing the reader to discern this for himself, rather than pointing out the obvious.

Papanoutsos conducts his discussion in terms of three specific examples. Account needs to be taken here of all three, in order to suggest the degree of generality which he would wish to claim for his thesis. Th examples are: (1) A real work of art not only is determined by the style of its period (or place of origin or school) but also determines that style. (2) In certain basic functions (from instinct up to perception) native forms both are the precondition of specific experience and are actualized by that experience. (3) In the evolution of living things it is those forms suitable for some purpose which prevail, but they do so not as the result of any purposeful activity.[59]

What is peculiar about these constructions, so that they can be worth discussion and analysis as a group? In each case there is clearly a certain tension between the two conjuncts. As Papanoutsos notes, there is no question of a logical contradiction between them; but it would seem that there is *something* irreconcilable about the two constituent propositions which makes their conjoint assertion a paradox at least. In the first example we appear to be saying that a cause-and-effect relationship holds convertibly between two terms. In the second it appears as if an a priori (or nativist) position and an a posteriori (or empiricist) one are so correlated that each, as Papanoutsos puts it, "owes its effectiveness to the other."[60] In the third example there is a strong suggestion of both coherence and a clash between two theoretical standpoints in biology, a finalist one and a mechanical. Papanoutsos insists that these constructions represent genuine paradoxes in thought, and not just in the expression of thought. They cannot be got rid of by mere rephrasing. Contrast, in this respect, the proposition, "Themistocles brought fame to Athens, but was himself made famous by it." This is no more than a rhetorically contrived way of saying something like: "Themistocles brought fame to Athens with his victories. Athens raised the reputation of Themistocles with the honors it paid him." But those other propositions express genuine quandaries of thought, attempts at an affirmation of truth bedeviled by inapposite concepts, or by ill-accordant modes of thinking, or by both. Such cruxes cannot be *rephrased* out of existence.

Yet the propositions concerned make sense, obliquely and enigmatically as they may do so. What Papanoutsos is arguing seriously is that they are markers of certain stages which have been reached by various branches of modern science; in the first example by the history and theory of civilization, in the second by psychology, and in the third by biology. If we wish to express in concentrated fashion what the scientific view of such and such a problematic situation amounts to, we sometimes cannot do better, in a way, than employ these paradoxes. For the scientific approaches, granted all their successes severally, have not been free of conflict. Nor are the concepts which we have at our disposal for the purpose of summarizing their results sophisticated enough to adumbrate how those theoretic elements which are at tension with one another may one day be developed so as to yield more adequate, fuller and more explicit solutions than are available to the human mind at this stage.

For example, we need something better than the concept of "determination" (representing conventional causality) when we attempt to express the two-sided dependence of product and productive source in proposition (1). In other terms, the notion of simple causality is too poor and too thin to do this work. That putting it to work produces a paradox as it does in proposition (1) is, however, of dialectical significance. Sooner or later, Papanoutsos thinks, the paradox should force us on to a more subtle and more comprehensive level of conceptual grasp. In proposition (2) the imperfection of the conceptual structure is similar, if not worse. As Papanoutsos puts it, neatly, "in this case it is not only the category of causality that labours, but also that of time."[61] What we lack here, and what in a dim way we must work conceptually toward is "a form of connection still more abstract (and more elaborate) than the two-sided causality of the previous example."[62] As for proposition (3), where the presence and the absence of "purpose" are both suggested, the inadequacy of the concept of "finality" (as for that matter of "mechanism") is painfully exposed. Somehow we need to transcend the level of which these tensions, and the insufficiently developed forms of thought associated with them, are characteristic.

Almost as an afterthought, but very interestingly, Papanoutsos remarks of the great traditional problem of freedom of the will that it too may be experienced as a form of conceptual cramp.

It is the same difficulty which confronts us when we try to accommodate moral freedom to natural necessity, not by ascribing to each its own sphere of jurisdiction but by regarding them as being, so to speak, interlaced within the same province of reality. We have to say that the will manifests itself in free actions within the concatenation of natural laws, although we are well aware that an order of things in which freedom (and for that matter natural law) is simultaneously present and absent, is an outrage to our thought and ways of speaking.[63]

Anyone who has had to present the problem of freedom of the will to undergraduate students of philosophy, or to students of any other kind for whom it may arise, will understand what it is to try to make this "outrage" in some fashion acceptable. It may be suggested indeed that the "interlacing" of freedom and necessity is probably the most outstanding example of all, within that category of paradoxical stances which interests Papanoutsos here, and which he thinks of the reasonable man as having to occupy—reluctantly, self-critically, and provisionally.

How provisionally, though? Papanoutsos's general diagnosis of the nature of the predicament which he is discussing is in effect that science, or at any rate the organized, disciplined investigation of the world around us, has outpaced philosophy, regarded as a vehicle for the representation of what science in general has achieved. He mentions the progress of research in bringing to light new material for investigation, the increasingly critical modes of evaluation of that material, and the increasing attention given to questions of scientific methodology. He is not suggesting that a "scientific" view of the world is destined to capture philosophy, or that philosophical insights are not, in turn, of concern to the scientist: the difficulty, however, is that philosophy has more and more to assimilate in the attempt to formulate and present a considered philosophical view of the world. Hence a philosopher's adoption of a "provisional" standpoint may be relatively permanent! The terms in which Papanoutsos spells this out are highly characteristic of him, and sound an appropriate note on which to end the present section. They begin with yet another paradox.

The need for transforming the basic forms of thought and the way in which this results in their continual renewal is both a precondition and an effect of scientific progress. It is convincing evidence against the view that theoretical reason is a system of rigidly fixed concepts and principles, given once for all so that the edifice of human knowledge may be constructed according to uniform rule. Reason is rather a capital which needs to be enriched and is being enriched continually, an equipment which needs to be supplied and is being supplied continually with new modes of apprehending and formulating the truth, step by step with improvements in means of research and changes in methodology. To remain unaltered is in no way essential to its functions of codifying and symbolizing, though the exceedingly slow rhythm with which it does change may give it the appearance of unalterability.[64]

The Criteria of Truth.   The discussion of *truth*, which was suspended earlier, may now be resumed. Attention has been drawn to Papanoutsos's equation of truth with an equilibrium between two demands, the one for maximum objectivity, and the other for the most perfect attainable organization in our theorizing. The problem left over was whether this equation does not commit him to a relativist (perhaps pragmatist) view of truth; or whether truth for him remains eternal verity, which we may keep on approaching but never reach. In *Gnosiology*, a little later,[65] Papanoutsos himself returns to the subject.

He allows himself a somewhat unusual latitude in his application of the term "truth." It is conventional to regard truth as being a perquisite of propositions (or perhaps statements or assertions), singly or in combination. But following his scheme of "gradations of knowledge," Papanoutsos is prepared to apply the term to a representation, a concept, an idea or a system as he understands these items. Any one of these can be either "true" or "false."[66] His elucidations are given in terms of adequacy, of the way in which these items variously meet (or fail to meet) his two fundamental and reiterable "demands." (The account given, the reader should be warned, is rather abstract.)

The first demand is met as follows. The requirement of the greatest attainable objectivity is one which can issue from the very top, as it were; that is, it can issue from some theoretical system down through its constituent "ideas," down through the concepts these embrace, down to the representations which the concepts purport to be all about. So: the general test is that within the system the "ideas" contained should be coherent with one another and should each have a contribution to make to the overall intellectual style and character of the system; within each "idea" the concepts which make it up should be coherent with one another, and none should be distorted in order to contribute to the whole; and each concept should have a clear and coherent field of application, in the representations which constitute its observational foundations. Here, then, is what Papanoutsos calls a "reference" of the system to the real world of which it treats.[67]

The second demand inverts this order of testing. The requirement of the most perfect possible organization is one which issues from the very bottom, as it were; that is, it issues from some representation or representations, through covering concepts, through the "ideas" into which these enter, up to the system the aim of which is to make coherent sense of them all. How is such and such a representation best, i.e., most clearly and unequivocally, covered at the conceptual level? What are the possibilities, as regards integration within an "idea," presented by the concept or concepts proposed? And how can the "idea" be accommodated most profitably and with the least contortion in a system that will be relatively all-explanatory? Here, then, is a "reference" in the other direction, of the observational and particular to some highly abstract and catholic intellectual construction.

The process of testing for truth, Papanoutsos insists, involves both of these references, of the higher to the lower and the lower to the higher. "Without reference to the immediately superior [cognitive level] and via it to the most superior, namely the system; and again without the corresponding reference to what is immediately lower, and via it to the lowest level, namely observation, the truth or falsity of an intellectual construct cannot be judged."[68] Unfortunately, Papanoutsos seems to have shifted his ground, if he means that this way of assessing the truth or falsity of something is *the* way, or a paradigmatic way, of doing so. For neither system nor representation can be made subject to such double reference. Only "ideas" and concepts can. And what counts as an intellectual construct? Surely a system does so, and even a representation, if my interpretation of Papanoutsos's "gradations of knowledge" is correct,[69] does so in a rudimentary way. But he cannot in consistency mean that we are unable to judge the truth or falsity of a system, or indeed of a representation. He says explicitly, just prior to the passage quoted, that we regard a representation as being true when it is observationally secured, and that for a system to be true it must at least not contort the

"ideas" which it accommodates.[70] He appears to treat such applications of "true" as being quite in order, and in any case they
are sanctioned by his own broad usage of the term which the
author has noted in introducing the present problem. So a certain
tension remains in his account. Is it that we have to envisage one-
way testing for truth (to put the matter colloquially) for systems
and representations as distinct from the two-way testing for truth
to which "ideas" and concepts may be subjected?

It is difficult to avoid the conclusion that, in spite of his
repeated emphasis on the crucial necessity of two-way testing,
Papanoutsos's real position is that there must be such a distinction. He makes the very significant remark that "it is customary
to regard now observation and now system as 'criteria of truth,'
since they constitute the two end-points of this scale [sc. the
gradations of knowledge]; that is, observation vis-à-vis the condition of objectivity judges but is not judged, and system vis-à-
vis that of organization likewise judges but is not judged."[71] It
is on these two insights, he notes, that extreme empiricism and
extreme rationalism base themselves, but unfortunately they
misuse them through metaphysical exaggeration. For neither objectivity alone nor perfect organization alone secures "the authority of " truth.[72] The objects of observation have to be assessed
from one standpoint—that of form, with reference to more and
more systematic considerations; the system has to be assessed
from another—that of content, with reference to more and more
objectively established representations. Obviously, neither can
be assessed from both standpoints. So again we seem to be landed
with an ambivalent view of what can be done to establish truth.
And it is a paradoxical and unsatisfactory one, for it amounts to
allowing that the two intermediate gradations of "knowledge"
can claim the accolade of truth in a way in which neither of the
others can do so. It is, of course, possible to be more confident
about particular constituents of a system than about the validity
of the system as a whole. But it does not appear that Papanoutsos
has this in mind. He says, enigmatically:

Observation is the starting-point and system the end-point in the progress of knowledge. Truth can be held to have been reached when knowl-

edge in its advance achieves a "closure," in which beginning and end "coincide." Then experience is elevated to Reason, and Reason descends to experience.[73]

It is after all at the level of "the system," he seems to be saying, that truth is to be located. Short of that, we must be dealing with what is relative and provisional only. If this is the position, it suggests that there can be no clear-cut answer to the question with which the present subsection began. This was the question whether Papanoutsos is committed to a relativist or to an absolutist view of truth. The author can suggest an answer only in terms such as he has used before: namely that from time to time Papanoutsos does look upon Truth as an "ideal of reason," but that as critical philosopher he has to allow that "truths" about the world, with which we have to do, cannot escape liability to review, and hence relativity. In other words, some features of his thinking—those contexts in which he is evaluating our actual and assessing our possible gnosiological achievements—are relativist in character; other features—contexts in which he is rather analyzing the philosophical idea of *gnosis* as such, are absolutist. So long as we remember that the word "truth" has, classically, appeared with or without a capital "t" according as *truth* is considered an ideal or an achievement, we should not be surprised that a treatise on "gnosiology" has regard to both standpoints. It is possible to occupy them both, though this cannot be done simultaneously.

The Epistemological Problem

"Internal" and "External" Controls on Theorizing.[74] From the "gnosiological" problem, with the main features of which the preceding chapter has dealt, Papanoutsos passes to the "epistemological," still on a fairly high level of abstraction. To be clear about the general order of his thinking, we need to advert once again to the difficult distinction between those two kinds of problem. It will be recalled that before ever he tackles the so-called "gnosiological" problem as such Papanoutsos applies himself to what he calls the "ontological," the problem of the general relationship of subject and object in knowledge. Having then dealt to his satisfaction with the gnosiological problem, beginning with the relationship of experience and reason, and using his analysis of this as a matrix within which to locate the criteria of truth, Papanoutsos turns to something which is (in a manner) more specific. The question with which he is now concerned is the identification, in the most general possible terms, of what contributes validity to knowledge, whether the knowledge be relatively theoretical or relatively pragmatic. We can recognize this as the (or, at any rate, a) leading question of "epistemology" as ordinarily understood.

Presented in these terms the order of discussion seems quite natural. But two things are liable to confuse the reader as to what Papanoutsos is about at certain stages. The first is that the three problems mentioned, "ontological" as well as "gnosiological" and "epistemological," are dealt with in a book called *Gnosiology*. The second is that the gnosiological problem is sometimes referred to by Papanoutsos as the "methodological" problem. The puzzlement thus caused can, perhaps, be mitigated if one tries to reexpress his three great preoccupations in the following summary terms. He begins with the distinction between what it is that knows and what it is that is known (or, between the intellectual powers of man and what it is that comes within the scope of these powers). He then considers the resources available to and the methods employed (or conceivably employable) by the intellectual powers—hence the intrusion, as remarked, of the word "methodological," about which no more than this need be said here. Third, he undertakes an analysis of what it is that makes human knowledge "good." To put the matter in a nutshell: the "gnosiological problem," in all its import, involves discussion of its parentage in the "ontological" and of its offspring in the "epistemological." Hence the bringing-together of the whole interconnected subject matter under the title *Gnosiology*.

In a way, what Papanoutsos is doing when he takes up his epistemological problem is to identify the two polarities which the author has noted in Papanoutsos's own thinking about truth, and to acknowledge their relative, their separately insufficient, character. (This makes his epistemology very much a detailed development of a feature of his gnosiology.) The general rubric under which he discusses the problem of epistemological validity is "Common Sense and Science." He is interested in the relationship of knowledge and practical purpose, the bearing upon this of the traditional idol of "pure" truth, and particularly the characterization of mathematical thinking and its value for knowledge of the world. In the investigation of these matters, Papanoutsos suggests, we again have to transcend (meaning, extract the best from) two dogmatic "antitheses,"[75] in this instance pragmatism—the view that truth is "merely" instrumental, is what works, what serves our purposes for the time being—and what he is willing to call "intellectualism"—the idea that somehow and in the end of the day, with desperate intensity, the mind can summon truth, constitute lasting truth about the world, from its own resources.

Part of what is involved in the "transcendence" of these two dogmas is the problem whether there is a hierarchy of kinds of truth, some perhaps being more stable, or more fertile, than others. To this problem there is no simple answer as Papanoutsos sees it. In a way, any "truth" is as good as any other, regardless of whether the properties or other aspects of things with which it is concerned are commonplace or arcane. Consider, for example, the question whether the molecular composition H_2O expresses the basic reality of water any more truly than the properties of dissolving sugar and quenching thirst—a question raised by William James and, when you put it like that, to be correctly answered in the negative. But such an answer is unsatisfying.

When we consider the distinguishing features of an object in relation to the consciousness which comes to "know" it, to give it categorial form as a construct of knowledge; when we proceed to compare them with one another as regards their *gnosiological* value, and assess them according to the standard, not of what brings us closer to the essence of the object . . . but of what gives us more accurate and fuller knowledge of it, what is most revelatory . . . of truth regarding it, then we shall be compelled to distinguish between them and to put them into some hierarchical order.[76]

What is "most revelatory" of truth is that feature or those features of whatever is in question that are the most susceptible of entering into and being interrelated in the most systematic, disciplined scheme applicable to such things. To return to James's example. Chemistry and common knowledge both have an interest in the properties of water. If we allow, as Papanoutsos assumes we must, that chemistry is more systematic and disciplined than common knowledge, then the molecular composition of water is more revelatory of truth about it than either its dissolving sugar or its quenching thirst. So we may say, alternatively: that there is a hierarchy of properties of water, and that in it the molecular composition of water ranks higher than these other two; or that there is a hierarchy of truths about water, in which the truth expressive of water's molecular composition ranks higher than those which have to do with water's "large-scale" effect on sugar or thirst. Papanoutsos, with Kantian austerity, prefers not to speak about the "inmost essence" of things; but if we are to indulge ourselves by doing so then, he insists, we shall speak sense only if by "inmost essence" we mean that feature or those features which are "gnosiologically prior"[77] in the manner just explained.

This answer to James's question, more qualified than and contrary in tendency to James's own, settles the issue in favor neither of pragmatism nor of intellectualism, but it contains suggestions of both. It is on the basis of hierarchical considerations such as those just mentioned, Papanoutsos observes, that scientific concepts are formed. In the process of forming and exploiting them, the mind neither regards the objective world without critical discrimination nor *imposes* its schemes on that world. There are in fact two general limitations on the mind's freedom to work out its interpretations of reality in any scientific terms.

First, there is no question of "arbitrariness" in the manner in which we undertake the work of intellectual "construction."[78] This represents an "internal" control upon the fashioning and development of our theories. In trying to find the most suggestive and fertile way of representing and explaining some particular area of investigation, the mind's freedom is limited by its dedication to order, the object of that dedication being the most complete, coherent, and consistent organization of the mind's constructs. What is correct in the "dogma" of intellectualism, namely its stress on perfection of intellectual form, is recognizable in and represented by such an objective. The topic is not altogether new; it is, in fact, a reappearance of one of Papanoutsos's "two demands," the demand for the most perfect possible intellectual organization, but now in explicit connection with the notion of "gnosiological value." In this context the term "perfect" is obviously to be defined, in large measure at any rate, by reference to mathematics and logic. Papanoutsos's views about these two topics will be reviewed in the following subsection.

The second general control consists in a policy of respect for the "objective basis" of our explanatory schemes. It represents an "external" check on our theoretical activity which corresponds, in this epistemological context, to the other of Papanoutsos's "two demands," the demand for the greatest attainable objectivity in our theorizing. For it is an almost constant question to what extent "things" themselves will endure those forms by means of which the mind would aspire to know its world. Hence our theorizing must rest also on "observation, and its methodical repetition, experiment."[79] And what is correct in the "dogma" of pragmatism, namely its stress on the workability of what we accept as true, is recognizable in and represented by this requirement.

Papanoutsos's investigation of "the epistemological problem" began with the question whether truth is essentially an instrument serving action or whether it can be the objective of a purely and strictly intellectual quest. His summary answer is that neither extreme, having it that thought is always one thing or the other, practically bent or theoretically bent, holds. Of course thought *can* serve action and it *can* be theoretically bent; but which of these obtains is a matter of emphasis, of the moment. What is more interesting than this blunt answer, however, is the gloss which Papanoutsos eventually puts on it. The following is a passage in which the emphasis tends to be against intellectualism, but in which the judgment is of a broad humanistic sort rather more characteristic of his other philosophical writings than of the austere *Gnosiology*.

As in its starting-point, its original postulates, so in its terminus, in the completion and crowning of its cognitive efforts, the human spirit cannot be confined within the narrow limitations of so-called pure reason, because then it would be, as it were, sentencing itself to inertia and sterility; as it were, clipping its own wings. Man takes possession of truth "with all his soul," and not only with the intellect. And the essence of the human spirit is freedom. Certainly the unconfined, anarchic arbitrariness, with which pragmatism would purport to credit it, is inadmissible. Just as illicit, however, is it to deny (as do the adherents of "intellectualism") the freedom of the human spirit, the formative impulse, the creative inspiration which characterizes it.[80]

Logic, Mathematics, and Knowledge of the World.[81]

Throughout the topics with which Chapter 3 has been concerned, Papanoutsos's preoccupation has been with human understanding, and mastery through understanding, of "the world." The dialectic, the intertwining, of theory and observation has been stressed increasingly as the account has progressed. In all this, the contribution of logic and mathematics to our knowledge of "the world" has rather been taken for granted. But if "intellectualism" is to have a footing anywhere, it is in these two fields of thought. Do they perhaps constitute schemes to which "the world" ("reality") cannot but conform, so that they are in the quite special position of being immune from one of the two kinds of verificatory check, the reference (one might almost say "deference") to experience, of which Papanoutsos makes so much in general terms? Or do even logic and mathematics observe a certain "respect for things"?

In the quoted passage with which the last subsection ended, Papanoutsos refers to the "formative impulse" of the human spirit; and if anything on the intellectual plane is relevant to that, logic and mathematics must be. We may therefore put the question what part logic and mathematics play in this connection; indeed, whether they have any part to play *other than* contributing to that impulse. The question is a topical one, particularly as regards mathematics. The status of "pure" mathematics, and the conditions of its applicability, are themes that have been much fought over in modern metatheoretical discussion; particularly since Einstein delivered himself of his famous dictum: "As far as the laws of mathematics refer to reality, they are not certain; and as far as they are certain, they do not refer to reality."[82] Papanoutsos's position in relation to these themes is interesting: it is Kantian in spirit, but worked out very much in his own manner. He mostly sidesteps the question whether the propositions of "pure" mathematics are "about reality" by claiming, and developing the idea, that they are essentially "productive,"[83] of propositions which manifestly *are* about reality—notably in the physical sciences. An attempt will be made in a moment to explain what this means. Perhaps more surprisingly, Papanoutsos thinks that the propositions of formal logic also are "productive," though it is questionable whether he has in mind precisely the same criteria of productivity as he has for mathematics.

It is sometimes urged that the "truths" of logic have necessity but not productiveness, since in the end of the day they turn out to be, if not axioms or postulates, then tautological transformations of or other tautology-producing kinds of operation upon axioms or postulates. Papanoutsos will not accept the emphasis thus put on "tautological," which he sees as distorting. In both truth-functional and class (etc.) logic, he affirms, the product of reasoning is "a new acquisition, a new conformation of the elements given in the premises, the logical founding of an affirmation, etc. So that the 'truths' of logic do have productiveness. But this virtue of theirs is very restricted in comparison with the productive capacity of mathematical propositions."[84]

In the light of this passage, that logic is "productive" *must* mean that those new forms of thought which it is the business of logic to work out help thought along: in the sense that, whatever thought be occupied with, logic can provide it with an indefinite variety of formal perspectives. The advantage of doing so—if there is more to the business than just ringing tautological changes on primary forms—must be the possibility (there is no necessity about it) that logical experimentation with the way in which we put things leads sooner or later to insight, enables us to *realize* something about the world which we had not realized, or had unclearly realized, before.

Why, however, does Papanoutsos think that the productivity of logical propositions is "very restricted" in comparison with that of mathematical? Sometimes he seems to be saying much the same thing about mathematical as about logical productiveness. Like Kant, he is impressed by the idea that in mathematics the mind "genuinely puts things together."[85] "The transition from one proposition to another . . . is not an apparent . . . but a genuine advance and signifies a new achievement, progress in our investigations."[86] It is not clear however, that more is meant by this than that in mathematics as in logic new conformations are achieved of elements that have appeared in some preceding form, and that this offers the possibility of enlightenment (about the world). But the mathematical context is different from the logical context. It is in a certain sense more substantial; it has a more particular content; the mathematical development of our thought can proceed to levels of precise insight that are inaccessible to logic. This may be what Papanoutsos has in mind when he says that in point of productivity mathematics is less restricted than logic. He does speak of "a world of forms" within which the transformations of mathematical analysis, as also the theorems of geometry, are a progressive disclosure of the detail.[87] But this world of forms cannot be reduced to a complex of purely "logical" elements: numbers, for instance, are neither classes nor classes of classes, as some logicians would have them to be, but "intellectual constructions specially elaborated."[88] Nor are mathematical forms "simply" abstractions from experience (though the "simply" seems to indicate that in some impoverished way they can be so regarded): rather, they are *"modes of relating* which raise the mind above the level of ordinary sensory insight and extend its theoretical activity."[89] The "special elaboration," then, is not confined to numbers, but applies to mathematical constructs generally. At the same time it provides a "quite particular grasping of reality by the theoretical consciousness," particular in what may be called its mathematical quality.[90]

How coherent is this account of mathematics? Apart from the difficulty, hinted at above, of regarding mathematical forms as being both abstractions and intellectual constructions, we now seem to be involved, after all, in thinking of even "pure" mathematics as being in itself "about reality." If the "special elaboration" is as described, does it not let in the danger that Papanoutsos, in indicating the general characteristics and the distinguishing features of mathematics, is trying to accommodate too many points of view? It seems certain that Papanoutsos would wish to claim that this is not true of his final, considered position. For the *obliqueness* of mathematics' concern with reality, originally mentioned as being characteristic of his view, is reiterated in the following summary, rather graphic, and very deliberate passage:

The value of mathematical science is to be found in the fact that it is a *systematic training of the mind,* a kind of methodical exercising of the intellect, the object of which is to increase the *possibilities of the mind's formative activity.* What we expect from this mental athleticism is that consciousness should develop its capacity for that great achievement: knowledge. Mathematics does not give us *knowledge,* but prepares our powers of thought for knowledge, so that thought can comprehend reality within its framework and explain it. What mathematics investigates and reveals is the great variety of rhythms in terms of which thinking can proceed and develop.[91]

As to the question raised in the first paragraph of this subsection, concerning the possible application to logic and mathematics of Papanoutsos's "two demands," construed as verificatory checks—it seems that logic and mathematics, as he sees them, fall outside the scope of these two demands. Neither the propositions of logic nor those of mathematics are *made good* by reference to experience. Those of logic, like those of mathematics, are "above the level of ordinary sensory insight."[92] It is possible to treat both kinds of proposition as "thought experiments," but this does not mean to say that they are "hypotheses" in any ordinary sense. They are, of course, susceptible to development in the way both of indefinite variation and of incorporation in indefinitely expandable schemes of (logical and mathematical) thought. But that is elaboration, not verification. Papanoutsos, in effect, regards each as an *organon,* so that each is quite special in our intellectual scheme of things. That their peculiar function is "productiveness" has to be construed with this consideration in mind.

Chapter Four

Moral Philosophy

Moral Theory and Moral Life

In a little essay in *Philosophical Problems*[1] Papanoutsos addresses himself to a popular misunderstanding about the nature and the potentialities of moral philosophy (or "ethics"). What is interesting in his discussion is not so much his recognition of this misunderstanding, which is familiar enough to philosophers, as his diagnosis of the reasons for it, and particularly of the reason why other main branches of philosophy are not subject to anything analogous.

He begins with the forthright declaration that on its ethical side "critical philosophy gives us the formal structure of virtue, and not the rule-book of the virtuous life."[2] (It may be remarked in passing that the identification of "virtue" as the central subject matter of ethics marks a very Greek approach.) When can a moral action be recognized as authentic and as being the product of a *positive* concern with a certain category of humanly encountered problems? That has to be the style of question with which ethics occupies itself, and not a preoccupation with the precise "content" of any action that one has to undertake in some difficult situation. Ethics offers us "analyses and elucidations . . . , not laws and precepts."[3] The tricky question, of course, is how to differentiate "form" from "content" for these purposes; and in particular, why it is necessary to disappoint the expectation that, having satisfied ourselves as to the formal criteria applicable to virtuous action of certain categories, we as theorists should be in a position to take a further step and to prescribe what action in particular, or at least what set of alternative actions, should be undertaken in concrete circumstances.

73

Papanoutsos here is much more concerned with the particular question just raised than to provide a specific analysis of the difference between form and content. As to this, he hardly goes further than to remind us that what is involved, in the determination of "form," is that the choice of an action should be made conscientiously, with sincerity, with an awareness of responsibility, and with regard to consistency. Now, of course, in the determination of form, undertaken as a philosophical objective in all possible conceptual fullness, there is much more to be said than that. What are the marks of conscientiousness, the tests of sincerity, the standards of responsibility, and the criteria of consistency as a norm in practical reasoning? Such questions must be raised, and such questions are undoubtedly still within the province of the moral philosopher. Suppose, however, that, as moral theorists, we contrive to answer them to our satisfaction. Why have we not yet made good a right to say: in circumstances *x* you ought to do *a*? Or rather, why have we not established a right to say this with complete specificity? Why does our jurisdiction fall short in principle of being an authority to validate *a* and not *b*, or *a* rather than *b;* or to put *a* and *b* into place in a scale of priorities such as to constitute some practical perspective for some agent? To questions of such a kind Papanoutsos offers three interconnected replies.

(1) There are various ways of setting oneself to pursue "the good," depending upon such personal factors as temperament and education, and such general factors as the cultural and spiritual climate of one's time and place. Enigmatically, Papanoutsos adds that there is but one way to pursue "the bad," and that is by the wholesale rejection of the good. But his main point is that to have positive moral quality an action must be performed in *freedom*. Principles of choice, initiative and imagination all come into the matter. A virtuous action is characteristically not stereotyped, as it would be if its content were derivable from the formal considerations of moral philosophy. Papanoutsos here seems to have in mind (very strongly) individual, personal morality as distinct from social morality, where some element of the stereotyped might have to be recognized. But here as elsewhere it

is the creativeness of moral life that preoccupies him. And "the good as spiritual creation prospers only in the context of freedom."[4] If moral philosophy could take the step from the *quality* to the *what* of moral action, it would turn us all into moral automata.

(2) It is to be recognized that a person's moral thinking and moral inclinations may be fashioned or sustained by the teaching of some outstanding, historic individual; so that the "principles" which that person accepts are identifiable as being of a type or kind. But, apart from the fact that these may be held more or less sensitively or critically—in other words, may themselves be a reflection of his freedom—their application remains a matter of judgment according to time and place. Again creativity is demanded if moral theorizing is to issue in personal moral decision. Such creativity seems to be for Papanoutsos—as "freedom" became for Sartre—a good in itself. He will not have it that there is any sense in comparing moral codes—granted that they are moral—with one another, or in looking for or toward the perfect moral code.

(3) A philosophical specialist in gnosiology would not be expected by a "pure" or "applied" scientist to prescribe what should go on in the scientist's laboratory or workshop. The philosopher's influence would extend no further than to encourage in the scientist a habit of reflectiveness about science and its methods. Nor would a philosophical aesthetician, however much he might encourage an artist to *think* about his art, be expected to try to teach him about points of style, methods of execution, or the manageability and virtues of specific artistic materials. What, then, is peculiar about a moral philosopher's situation, so that he is expected, not uncommonly, to go so far as to issue precepts, admonition or advice? The peculiarity, Papanoutsos observes, is simply that the world into which he is expected to extend his activities is a nontechnical one, unlike that of the scientist, or the artist. These deploy special technical knowledge and special technical skills which quite obviously debar interference by a philosopher as such. But the ordinary man with his moral problems has no such technical fence. Why should the wisdom of the

moral philosopher *not* produce definitive solutions to moral problems and clear guidance in the working out of the ordinary man's moral projects? If in these matters the moral philosopher is not competent to judge, who is competent?

Such is the rationale behind the misplaced expectation with which Papanoutsos is concerned. But, as he implies, it is faulty. Too much is made of the fact that the ordinary man, unlike the scientist or the artist, does not possess a technical armory which can hold off the philosopher as such from legislating for him. What is crucial to Papanoutsos's thinking, it appears, is the consideration that instead of a technical armory the ordinary man possesses something which is, in its way, just as impenetrable, namely his freedom. The moral responsibility of the individual exists in and through that freedom: only the individual, with the sensitivities which he has developed through his own trial and experience, can be the final judge of what exactly he is to do, as a moral agent, when and where. Philosophers may try to understand such judgments, down to the last detail, retrospectively or in prospect; but they may not legislate for them, without destroying what they are trying to understand.

Freedom: An Analysis

The preceding section has brought to the forefront the notion of *freedom,* and in association with it, that of *creativity.* Throughout his main works Papanoutsos dwells frequently upon those two linked notions which, for him, express man's greatest possibilities, and his glory. He regards freedom not, in a Sartrian spirit, as a human predicament, but rather as a human capacity which we have to cultivate, and have to strive to fulfill. If Papanoutsos, like Aristotle, were to allow himself to speak in terms of man's *ergon* (or "function"), he would probably identify that *ergon* as freedom-in-exercise, rather than as the exercise of contemplation subserved by a decent moral life in which Aristotle would have it consist. Papanoutsos is second to none in his devotion to rationality, the reason upon which contemplation is founded; but if we are to think in terms of the end for man, or perhaps the complete fulfillment of man's function, then rationality is not enough. As he says at the end of *Gnosiology:*

> Living man and his conscious world make up a whole of many aspects, profoundly interconnected. We can indeed distinguish, as founts of value, the true, the good, the beautiful and the sacred; and correspondingly, systematic thought, morality, art and religion as special functionings of spiritual life. But, as a concrete existent, man participates in all of these and cannot give himself to one while letting the others go completely dead within him. The "believer," the "savant," the "man of virtue," the "artist" are logical abstractions, not living forms of human existence.[5]

Perhaps this is an overstatement. One has seen some of these "logical abstractions" around. But it may be agreed that the norm for human living is as Papanoutsos says. Creativity and freedom are no less possible, and no less fulfilling, in one dimension than in others of those named.

So much for Papanoutsos's general stress on the human importance of "freedom." A close philosophical analysis of the concept, however, is another and more difficult matter. Papanoutsos provides this in a study called "The Problem of Freedom" which first appeared in his *Philosophy and Education* in 1958.[6] His method of approach is phenomenological.

There is a remarkable stubbornness, he observes, about the human conviction of freedom or free will. (For present purposes these terms may be used interchangeably.) This is due importantly to the fact that the persuasion of "freedom" is part and parcel of something lived through—the almost untranslatable Greek term is *vioma*—while what may be called subverting considerations are the product of theory. Unlike the former, which is an "immediate" experience frequently renewed, the latter (the theory) is impersonal and "distanced." It is not that this particular experience is something which, like Hume's "idea of ourselves," or Sartre's admit-it-or-not awareness of freedom, we can never catch ourselves without. Frequently renewed though it be, it is also part of a relatively crucial kind of experiencing which makes up but one, a particularly "impressive," sector of our existence.

Papanoutsos describes the experience of freedom as a sentiment of accountability going along with a certain self-criticism, with which we surround an initiative of any consequence, whether before or, perhaps more commonly, after the event. In taking such an initiative we feel ourselves to be both responsible and accountable for the action in question, "responsible" in terms of psychological explicability and "accountable" in those of moral assessability. Papanoutsos says firmly, but without arguing the matter, that personal responsibility and accountability are interdependent concepts, and hence that there is at least an overlap between psychological and moral freedom. In explicating *freedom* questions of "good" are relevant, in that the self-criticism referred to involves the question, "What is 'the good of ' this thing which I have done, am doing, or am about to do?" "The good of it" is something which I have taken, am taking, or am about to take it upon myself to realize. So appears the experience of freedom when regarded from a general phenomenological standpoint.

This analysis of what the so-called "experience of freedom" is like may ring true; but it cannot avert the question whether there is any more to *freedom* than that felt quality of certain decisions, or actions as the case may be, of being somehow crucial. As Papanoutsos himself puts it, the question is whether the analysis discloses any more than the circumstance that man thinks he is free, whereas "freedom" as such is an illusion. Is the sentiment of freedom, then, as far as we can get? Is the concept of freedom really resistant to being "analyzed away"?

Dubiousness of this sort is nurtured by two general, and more or less "popular" arguments against freedom of the will. Papanoutsos meets these head on, before he proceeds to give his own circumstantial account of how freedom is to be "located." The first contrary argument is that the whole idea of freedom of the human will comes into conflict with that of natural law; and so well established is the latter that the former cannot stand up against it. This, says Papanoutsos, is just wrong. There is nothing in natural law to conflict with man's being responsible and accountable for his decisions, in particular those made with serious deliberation and intent. What does so conflict is not "natural law," but a certain theoretical hypothesis about nature, namely an all-embracing determinism which is anticipatory and stipulative, and which has no claim to be revelatory.

The second contrary argument is not altogether different from the first, but Papanoutsos's reply to it is of a different sort. It is often felt that freedom of the will is in conflict with a principle which modern science can rightly claim to be a most fertile one, namely that man is the product of his physical, psychological and social conditions. If this is accepted comprehensively then, it would appear, those actions which we call free are merely those which we are not yet, for technical reasons, in a position to predict. Papanoutsos, however, denies that the difficulty here *is* a technical one, and not a matter of principle. He expresses his denial in a slightly curious, but nonetheless powerful way. No matter how advanced our science, he suggests, "all we could succeed in predicting would be a *possibility,* never an *actual* decision prior to its manifestation."[7] That is, even though we got it right, it would be qua possibility that we predicted the decision and *never* infallibly. Like Sartre, Papanoutsos writes (unsympathetically) about the intersection of natural laws by means of which we may hope to "capture" some decision or action; but also like Sartre, he holds that no such network is ever so close as to constitute a decision trap (or action trap). He gives his reason for this view in crucial general terms which he will then strive to make good in detail:

Between them [sc. possibility and reality] there is always a gap: this is where freedom obtains. Man is properly to be termed free for this reason: that he alone has the power . . . to convert—to the extent and in the manner that he judged opportune or correct, advantageous or right—possibility into reality, and out of the "plurality" of probable outcomes (such being what the polynomial of scientific prognosis always yields) to realize the "singularity" of the definitive act of will.[8]

In what does this definitive act of will consist? Consider the position of an outside observer (a scientific one) who is attempting to study someone else's "mental processes" as being likely to lead to some crucial decision, and to anticipate that decision if he can.

What does he have to go upon? His study of the situation will have disclosed a complex of conditions, biological, psychological, sociological, and so on, each of them relevant in that it will have some tendency to come into the subject's reckoning, and the sort of bearing of which upon prospective outcomes is (let us allow) well established. These considerations will not just be a set of "factors affecting" but, it is to be presumed, will amount to something more. The scientific observer is bound to have a view as to how they relate to one another, what their relative weighting is, and what outcome to expect on this basis. According to Papanoutsos, however, he can do no more than offer a prospective simulation of what is to happen. His own evaluation, from a scientific point of view, of the relevant conditions is quite other than a fiat (Papanoutsos's term in this context). The fiat, which is always required (of the subject), is also always in question.

> The conditions perceptible to the outside observer . . . which tend to bring about the effect, are not its cause, since the internal process which will terminate in the definite decision (the moment of *fiat!*) and which will show how these factors have been put in order and given precedence, has not yet been completed. I mean that the decision, by assigning "position" and "value" to each condition (this burden of responsibility being essentially freedom), transforms a series of abstract possibilities (probable causes) into a single, formally unified, definite, actual cause.[9]

Papanoutsos takes as a concrete example the dossier which might be compiled by an anthropologist carrying out a systematic study of a certain turbulent individual, whose future is highly likely to be troubled and is therefore a matter for special concern. The records of the subject's history, personality, etc., which the anthropologist assembles—Papanoutsos exemplifies them at length—are as comprehensive as his scientific experience and training can make them. Eventually he concludes that this individual, if he becomes subject to given pressures, will either commit a violent crime or kill himself. "I make no difficulty," says Papanoutsos, "about admitting that, occasionally, forecasts of this kind are confirmed to a remarkable degree. . . . But I shall not be puzzled in the least to learn that our expert . . .

has been proved wrong in his forecasts: that suddenly the living subject of his experiment, instead of committing a murder or killing himself, went through a religious crisis and secluded himself in a monastery."[10]

Why should the expert not have forecast *this?* Well, he might have done so, but still it would have represented only one possibility among others. Papanoutsos's line of argument, it may be repeated, is that since the fiat is not the expert's, the expert's prognosis is always, in principle, fallible. But cannot the nature of the fiat itself come within the scope of what the scientist can know, prospectively, about the individual? Papanoutsos does not put this key question in so many words, but it is clear that his answer must be "no." The nature of the fiat, he allows, can be known *retrospectively.* The context in which a causal account of the subject's whole performance can be admitted *is* the retrospective: that is, it can there be admitted as definitive, as being no longer limited to possibility. We tend to think of the scientific prediction of human actions as acquiring, in optimum conditions, parity of status with retrospective explanation; but this is a mistake. It is also a mistake to think that because actions can be explained retrospectively, they therefore were not freely performed. The causality involved in such explanations is not "mechanical," not even "physical," according to Papanoutsos, but what he calls "historical."[11] This is causality in a very broad sense of the term, embracing motive, intention, etc., as not-further-reducible "causal" factors. Thus, the actual "free" performance now comes into the account, but without any transmogrification of its deliberative, considering, evaluative character in virtue of which we call it "free." (Much may be said about deliberation, consideration and evaluation in the "causal" terms of this or that special science, but that is another story which [Papanoutsos would probably claim] does not affect the present issue.)

The paragraph with which Papanoutsos concludes this particular discussion is both summary and pregnant, and is worth quoting in full:

The foregoing analysis has shown that there is nothing contradictory or paradoxical in the proposition: "While human decisions (according to the free-will doctrine) cannot be foreseen with certainty, nevertheless (in accordance with the theory and practice of science) they can be explained satisfactorily, once they have been revealed." For *prediction* and *explanation* do not mean the same, and are not equipollent: prediction does not constitute explanation, and explanation does not presuppose [successful] prediction. Each of them is sought and achieved on a special level of enquiry, with its own data and its distinctive perspective; although in each case the mind works on the same logical principle, the principle of sufficient reason. Our conclusion, therefore, is that the admission of free will does away not with the principle of causality but with the hypothesis that there is only one kind of causality, the *physical* (the status of which, in any case, has been thrown in question by contemporary science). As we have seen, there is also *historical* causality: and with it the idea of freedom is perfectly consistent. [12]

This philosophical analysis of the concept of freedom is, in fact, posterior to Papanoutsos's larger-scale treatment of freedom as creativity, a supreme value in the arts—his views on which have yet to be discussed—the moral life and the intellectual life of man. It is of some interest to ask whether the analysis reflects back on and illuminates this treatment significantly. It may be claimed to do so much inasmuch as it clarifies the idea of "taking an initiative." The creator of a work of art, a moral or religious reformer, the exponent of a fertile new theory or style of thinking, all "initiate" in that some new principle or way of seeing things, an *archē,* is, in a sense, "in them" and underived. Papanoutsos's example serves to illustrate this perhaps more clearly in the moral sphere than in the others. He speaks, significantly, of "the order in which the initiative of the person concerned allowed them [sc. the various necessary conditions of the decisive action] to influence the result." [13] In this way he strives to give meaning to the notion of moral decisiveness, which in relatively important circumstances could amount to moral creativity, "within" the agent. In explaining creativity in the arts and in systematic theorizing the notion of "ordering" may tell less of the story. But it does tell an important part of the story, in terms perhaps of a form which is in no sense imposed, but which comes into being only finally, as the final expression of what an artist or a theorist makes of the more or less recalcitrant materials or ideas that are his to "compose."

Morality and Personal Freedom

Papanoutsos's emphasis on freedom and creativity as being features of our *moral* achievements is intensified when he comes to consider the topic of "social" morality (sometimes, as he says pejoratively, "social automatism") and others taken as linked with it, namely moral life generally, moral conflict, and the attainment of virtue.[14] Beginning with a sociological review of the nature and the rationale of social morality, he proceeds to expose the insufficiency of social morality as a code for the conduct of life at a certain level of thoughtfulness and earnestness. He moves in the direction of a personalism which recognizes, in morality as in art and theoretical activity, the possibility of a creative insight or style of thinking, exercised in freedom but against a disciplined background, which makes supreme virtues, each of its own kind but still having some affinity with one another, out of the moral life, the artistic life, and the life dedicated to theoretical understanding. The ancient Greek concept of virtue, *aretē*, "excellence," is very much with us in this context, though artistic virtue or excellence now takes more of a place, along with moral and intellectual virtue, than it tended to do in ancient times.

In showing that a social morality is necessary to any form of tolerable social existence, that indeed it is part of what constitutes a human society, Papanoutsos writes fairly and not without sympathy for his subject, and it is not necessary here to recapitulate this part of his work. Why, then, does he apparently alter his stance, and proceed to write as if social morality were merely a matrix in which morality of a more vital and critical sort could come into being and develop? The change is marked by an abrupt (and strictly an inconsistent) terminological shift within the course of two sentences. The main principle of social morality, he points out, is that of reciprocity, to the effect that one should not do to others what, in comparable circumstances, one would not wish to have done to oneself. This seems to cover a great deal, in the way of safeguards against falsehood, perjury, theft, murder, and so on, a whole complex of restraints and associated ways of behaving the rationale of which is to secure an orderly, peaceful coexistence of a man with his fellows. But from another point of view it covers very little: the *scope* of moral life is much greater than this principle suggests. "The moral life of men," Papanoutsos is therefore led to say, "is not confined within the narrow circle of these concerns. On the contrary, if one takes a closer look at it one is persuaded that it begins precisely where the limits are reached of moral values formed under social pressure."[15] So there is morality and *morality;* and from this point onward it is *morality* (or personalized morality) in which Papanoutsos mainly interests himself.

This terminological ambivalence is unsatisfactory, however, because in giving a rounded account of the moral life there can be no question of dismissing social morality completely from the reckoning. Papanoutsos himself does not do so. For one thing, there must remain some element of social morality in one's moral code as a whole. For another, it is against a background of difficulties (inconsistencies perhaps) and insufficiencies in social morality that the need arises to work out for oneself what is good, right, incumbent, and so on. Inert, prosaic, standardized, even stifling, one may find social morality, in certain of its aspects, to be. But in a curious way even these features are "dynamic." Some moral initiative is demanded of any soul whom they make restless. Over against them a person has spiritually to assert *himself,* and to be at one and the same time both responsible and creative.

Who, apart from such obvious examples as Socrates, Christ, and the Buddha, are the saints or heroes who could respond to such a demand? Papanoutsos seems to come and go on the question how common an experience answering a real moral challenge is. He conveys the impression at one stage that it occurs less rarely than we may think. For, apart from the "greats," he remarks, there are also the more modest heroes of moral life.[16] Their work has the same essential characteristics, which Papanoutsos makes a considerable point of stressing, as those of more celebrated reformers. Like the latter, they act freely, responsibly, and creatively. But their impact is less, because for one reason or another they tend to keep quiet about the nature of their conflicts and achievements. Unfortunately, this relatively "catholic" view of the distribution of authentic morality is difficult to square with the remark, also made by Papanoutsos, that morally free and creative men are in a very small minority, and that life provides, for the exceptional individual, few moments in which he can be deeply aware of the feeling of spiritual freedom. [17] Again, it is observed in a later discussion that "moral consciousness rarely and with difficulty attains to self-containedness and self-sufficiency."[18] But—and this consorts rather oddly with the earlier assertion that moral heroism is by no means always articulate—once it does so, it assumes a missionary character. The moral man who has broken through regards it as his *duty* to teach. "Moral activity as such, as [properly] spiritual activity, has a tendency to transcend the boundaries of individual life and by teaching and example to become an object of interest to and concern for collective."[19]

It would be inappropriate to make too much of these tensions in Papanoutsos's thinking. They may be more apparent than real; but it is difficult to resolve them, partly because his discussion suffers from the absence of specific examples of what taking the initiative in moral activity consists or would consist in. Basically, Papanoutsos has to reconcile two points of view, not in themselves inconsistent but still requiring a fine balance to be maintained between them. The first is that in conscientious moral activity, as in aesthetic activity, man achieves a particular and precious kind of freedom. In each case this freedom is something to be gained through more or less intense, "spiritual" striving: it is not a gift or endowment. The second is that, nevertheless, such freedom is not the prerogative of an elite; it is at least within the sights of people generally. Papanoutsos's unquestionable humanitarianism (in this context perhaps a more apt term than "humanism") licenses us, it may be allowed, to treat with some reservation those remarks (some of which have been noted) that might suggest otherwise. What it comes to is that he is entitled to remind us, in one way and another, that even weak human beings may have their moments of moral heroism, and even morally heroic human beings may have their moments of human weakness. In any case the apex of morality, for Papanoutsos, consists in making certain moral principles responsibly *our own;* through spiritual struggle conferring an authority upon them, and not subscribing to them submissively as to a set of "laws" external to ourselves.

The Morally Problematic

The author remarked in the last section, when outlining Papanoutsos's views about *personal* morality, on the absence—in the immediate context—of illustrations of what it is to take the initiative morally. Moral freedom, creativity, and associated notions like responsibility, figured in a general, schematic way only. Elsewhere, however, as in an essay entitled "The Morally Problematic" of which some account should now be taken,[20] Papanoutsos does bring out the complexities of moral life as it is lived. Here he indicates the sort of setting, or at any rate one sort of setting, in which there is scope for free, creative and personally responsible moral decision. The question will emerge, however, where we are to look for criteria according to which such decision can claim justification.

Papanoutsos is thinking of situations in which one is trying to act with total conscientiousness, to satisfy one's sense of responsibility up to the hilt and in the process to see with maximum clarity what factors are involved and how they are to be measured against one another. (He remarks, again, that this sort of attitude is the only one worthy to be deemed "moral": once again "social" morality is implied to be only the substratum of moral life.) The object of the essay is to show how, quite typically, circumstances may frustrate such conscientiousness. The rules and principles on which it endeavors to work may not "take care of" all the circumstances in which a decision has to be made. If they have to be qualified in order to do so, the effect may be to leave us in a quandary how to act, whether in one way or in a more or less contrary way. Is it, then, that in the end of the day we may be left with nothing but good will to claim credit for? (And, if this is so, what scope has there been for creativity in our moral thinking and acting? The uneasy question about criteria with which [as remarked above] Papanoutsos's discussion may leave us repeats itself in such terms.)

The examples on which Papanoutsos works are, very summarily, as follows:

(1) Prior to a period of absence an acquaintance may leave me with a quantity of valuables to keep for him until his return. I accept this charge. During his absence I discover that he has obtained the valuables by misappropriation or by other morally objectionable means. Do I fulfill the trust he placed in me or do I take steps to see that the valuables are not returned to him as unquestionable possessions? Am I to take account of other people in a way which I did not originally intend?

(2) Is one to tell the truth without distortion, without reservation, in various easily imaginable, distressing circumstances: as in communicating the full diagnosis of a child's illness to a mother perhaps fatally unable to accept it; or in allowing the children of a condemned criminal to get to know of their parent's execution before rather than at some time after the event?

(3) A legal representative of a defrauded trader may discover in the course of his investigations that, while the trader was undoubtedly defrauded, the circumstances of the fraud were so "mitigating" that the case begins to look distorted. Has the representative any option but to carry out his brief, his professional duty, to the full, and to leave it at that?

(4) If a person begins to suspect, after a series of acts of charity toward a certain individual, that his charity is being "taken advantage of " and not being turned to good account, is he (uneasily, perhaps) to cut that individual off without further benefaction—to say that charity stops here?

In each of these instances the perplexity of the person called upon to make a decision is that of determining his own moral horizon: "it is not at all certain whether obeying the rule, in that particular configuration of circumstances which the course of events has cast up, is doing what is right, what is morally blameless."[21] Papanoutsos is at pains to point out that we are not dealing here with a "conflict of duties" or with a "crisis of conscience" in an associated sense. He does not see the problem as one of reconciling two equally demanding but intransigent duties. In each instance what the agent is preoccupied about centrally is *one* moral rule, a rule which comes to the forefront in certain circumstances, but which turns out to seem insufficiently adaptable to those circumstances. It does so in the sense that its application *could* be more productive of (moral) harm than of good, that the results *could* be (morally) "unfitting."[22]

At this stage the sensitive agent will begin to think "dialectically" about his predicament.[23] The handing back of the valuables, it now appears, is and is not the fulfillment of a trust. It seems as if one respects and does not respect the truth by telling it to people in a certain position. It looks to be a matter of keeping and not keeping a "promise" given, if one thinks of representing a client when the background in his case emerges in a certain way. It is and is not, apparently, helpful to a particular individual to receive charity according to his (genuinely recurrent) needs. The sensitive agent thus vacillates between affirmation and denial of the principle at issue. As Papanoutsos puts it in reference to the agent's moral consciousness, "he denies not the necessity but the sufficiency of its deontological capital."[24]

There is no question, then, of the agent's not accepting the moral rules in question in a general way. They are, as has just been said, part of his deontological capital. But it is a matter of judgment—to put the situation no more strongly—whether to let them apply *here* and *now*. This is where the agent's responsibility *has* to be exercised, where his freedom is inescapable, and where whatever he decides becomes, after its fashion, a pattern, for better or for worse. (The thinking here is extremely reminiscent of that of Sartre in "Existentialism and Humanism," but it is more than likely that Papanoutsos has made his own way to this point.) For there is no guarantee that the agent's decision, in such a situation, is right. Perhaps the end to which his decision will be a means will *not* be a desirable one; perhaps the duty which he finds incongruous was more imperative than he reck-

oned; perhaps the virtue which he sees his decision as exempli-
fying, or the *style* of decision which he prefers will wear thin;
and so on. Perhaps he has made a mistake, indeed, in letting one
of these "models"—the means-end one, the deontic one, etc.—
dominate his thinking to too great an extent; he has not seen,
perhaps, in what a complex way the models may relate to one
another in practice; or he has seen; and the complexity has defeated
him.

Thus the agent finds himself in a situation where there *are*
criteria bearing on his decision, but he cannot be sure of them,
of how far they extend or of how they may be connected with
one another. His decision thus becomes, in a sense, a hostage to
fortune: its pattern will stand the test of time, or it will not.
One would like to feel, of a work of "creation," that it had firmer
prospects of survival than such considerations as these may suggest. Risk is perhaps more a feature of moral than it is of artistic
creativity. Certainly Papanoutsos is under no illusions as to the
extent to which an individual's moral judgments *are* at risk. "This
[the sort of considerations just outlined] explains why moral life
is so agonized; many moral problems are not simply hard to solve,
but are insoluble."[25] He does not mean, however, that in the sort
of cases he has been examining we are bound to act without any
rationale whatsoever. An agent's decision may be very much a
matter of "taking the plunge," but *ex hypothesi* it is still a decision
according to *some* principle which can be argued about and
assessed.

Humanism and Reason

In Papanoutsos's ethical writings it is often difficult to discern
a clear distinction between moral theory (i.e., the critical analysis
of moral systems and moral judgments), moral sociology, moral
phenomenology, and moral psychology. This is a feature of but
not necessarily a fault in his ethical thinking. He is interested
in morality as a dimension of human culture, extending from the
collective, habitual and more or less codified type which the
author has been calling social morality, to the individual, relatively tentative, self-aware, self-critical, and "open" personal

morality which Papanoutsos obviously regards as the apex of
moral life, and which, precisely because it is "open," is (as we
have seen) difficult to typify. It is adventurous without being
irresponsible, is sensitive to the *problems* of conduct and is anti-
pathetic to any suggestion of dogmatism in the settlement of
them. What interests Papanoutsos is the sort and style of person
in whom such values can be encountered. And he insists that for
such a person more, far more, is involved in the business of
scrupulous living than "knowledge," or a single-minded devotion
to reason, whether "pure" or even, as some have understood it,
"practical." To use old-fashioned terms, the nature of moral problems has to be understood with reference not only to the intellect,
but also to the will and the emotions, people's desires and sentiments, and so on. Hence the idea of a moral calculus has no
attraction for him; the logic of this or that actual or possible
moral code has a strictly limited interest; and the points of view
of those moral philosophers who see in the "rationale" of moral
attitudes nothing but what belongs to "reason" he subjects to
severe criticism. It is not surprising, then, that in his ethical
writings there should be the continuum of approaches remarked
on above.

This helps to explain also why in his *Ethics* there should be so
much emphasis as there is on historicophilosophical criticism.
Papanoutsos holds seriously that moral philosophy has become
distorted because so many of the great figures in its history have
set themselves to show that what is fundamental to morality is
getting things right in a certain fashion; that is, that moral rectitude
is an achievement of the intellect, of more or less strenuous
thought in which what is involved is nothing but *rational* considerations. For their one-sidedness in this respect Papanoutsos
criticizes, at length, Socrates, Plato, Descartes, Spinoza, and Kant
among others. All of these, he thinks, fail in their various ways
to allow that "the moral consciousness has breadth and depth
greater than the narrow sector of our internal life controlled by
Reason."[26] It is not, of course, that these great thinkers have
failed to illuminate the moral life, have failed altogether to show
what sort of struggle it is. But sometimes their success has de-

pended on their importing and exploiting considerations such as do not follow from, and cannot be analyzed into, strictly reason-given elements recognized in their systems. Possibly the clearest example of such heterogeneity is Spinoza, with whose "geometrical" method Papanoutsos explicitly contrasts his own dialectical one.

Spinoza ordered his whole system of "truths" about the moral constitution of man and of norms appropriate to it, from successive sets of definitions and axioms, supplemented at places by more or less plausible postulates, from which he argued to "demonstrated" results with what purported to be complete, formal, logical rigor. As an intellectual achievement his system is unique—and majestic. But it is subject, on "systematic" grounds, to a major criticism. It claims definitively to elucidate the force of the moral "ought," the concepts of right and wrong, good and bad, and associated notions, using only "truths of reason" (which are in the last resort axiomatic in nature), plus other principles (the postulates), which although "factual" purport to be true uncontroversially. Papanoutsos, for one, would hold that this program puts too much emphasis on "intellectual" intuition or insight, the mere ability to "see" the structure and the interrelationships of what, in one way or another, simply "is" or "is not" the case in this world. If Spinoza, for example, succeeds in saying things both powerful and persuasive about the norms applicable to human conduct, he does so because he relies on more than cold reason in presenting them. Not just intuition, but evaluation: such might be an appropriate reminder to any philosopher who sets himself to delineate and to elucidate the moral dimension in human thinking and conduct. Papanoutsos goes so far as to claim that Spinoza's greatness as a moral philosopher lay importantly in the *breach* of strict rationalism represented by his introduction of ideas such, for example, as those of man's *conatus*—that is, his constant striving to preserve and maintain his own being—and of his capacity to give life, as it were, to knowledge, in a final coming to terms with the world and himself which Spinoza called "the intellectual love of God." Whether these ideas are supportable or not, they do invite ethical exploitation—and from Spinoza they receive it. But they are not derived in any combinatory or analytical way from the primitive terms of the system, nor do they emerge as the fruit of its axioms. They belong to its really very important postulational element. Papanoutsos observes that they betray on Spinoza's part an intuitive awareness of the anemic and barren character of the traditional rationalism which he himself had in fact set out to reform, develop, and perfect. They are, indeed, "robust and fruitful ideas drawn from his own human experience and the metaphysical yearning within him."[27] With such new elements as that of the *conatus* Spinoza "grafted the tree of ethical rationalism"[28]—but he thereby diminished most significantly the homogeneity of his system.

This paraphrase of Papanoutsos's critique of Spinoza may suggest that Papanoutsos is in the paradoxical position of being impelled by his own respect for reason toward a considered ethical antirationalism which has more than a little affinity with David Hume's provocative thesis that "reason is, and ought only to be the slave of the passions, and can never pretend to any other office than to serve and obey them."[29] It is preferable to say that Papanoutsos's attitude to reason cannot be understood except as part and parcel of his "humanism," the respect for and ultimate faith in man in all of his potentialities which Papanoutsos's ethical thinking, particularly the book called *Ethics,* manifests from start to finish. Such humanism involves no easy optimism; the faith *is* "ultimate." In particular, "reason" is seen in its full human context, which is to say that it is not taken in artificial abstraction, as an autonomous *organon* for the determination of acceptable ethical principle—the status accorded to it, in Papanoutsos's estimation, by traditional rationalism. So humanism of Papanoutsos's type involves a certain loss of expectation as to what reason can do on its own, and this has implications for the general question of method in moral philosophy; it helps to explain why Papanoutsos adopts a dialectical and sometimes circuitous-looking approach to his representation of human morality.

Spinoza, by contrast, was pursuing a kind of finality, on two planes—that of achieving a clear and distinct understanding of the meaning of ethical concepts, and that of being certain how to act and what to aim at in terms of these concepts. Such a pursuit—to interpret Papanoutsos rather freely at this point— is really a rare self-indulgence when seen in the context of man's historical struggle to achieve any sort of moral-philosophical understanding, and to acquire any sort of certainty in matters of moral touch. The object of that struggle is not attainable, on either level, by reliance on one's own pure, austere reason alone: on the first level, because the exploration of ethical ideas involves all the ins and outs, the considerations and the counterconsiderations, the multiplicity of points of view with which the progress of philosophy has left us—Spinoza did his best to be a counterexample, but he did not succeed; and on the second level, because moral life typically is a struggle with perplexity—at any rate, moral life at its most self-conscious and sensitive. Whatever be the correct account, then, of the relationship between moral philosophy and moral life, neither can achieve the finality which Spinoza sought—assuming, that is (as Papanoutsos believes), that Spinoza's attempt was a salutary failure. We shall get nearer to the truth of things, complex, untidy, opaque, and difficult to formulate as that may be, by adopting another method than the "geometrical." Where moral philosophy is concerned, we need to follow the twists and turns which argument has taken over the ages, and to be sensitive to the degrees of contrariety that are to be found in more or less contemporary discussion. In other words, the truth has to be accumulated painfully and piecemeal, through indefinitely continued human argument. It is not there "to be found," so that at a certain stage we may claim the role of gnostics. And where the business of moral living is concerned, we need to see that there is an individual freedom to question, and thereby to *put* in question, the jurisdiction of any particular moral principle or set of moral principles over what has morally to be assessed and morally to be dealt with.

Hence Papanoutsos's preference, in philosophizing about morality, for a dialectical method, as being particularly appropriate to the inescapability of moral problems, and to human involvement in both their genesis and their solution. Hence also his refusal to lay down the law in any respect when considering particular examples of moral predicaments (such as were taken for discussion in the preceding section): in each instance his unwillingness to endorse either of two contrary ways, or even to propose a compromise way, of emergence from the apparent moral impasse which he has described is noteworthy. Good will, conscientiousness, respect for rules, freedom, creativity—all these factors enter into his diagnosis of what the moral agent is involved with, and of the attitudes which he can adopt in his involvement; but what, in any particular case, they issue in is not a matter for legislation by the philosopher. Quite possibly—and this Papanoutsos does admit in the Prologue to his *Ethics*—a philosophical cast of mind or a systematic training in philosophy may improve the quality of our moral thinking, but it will never provide it with a decision procedure.

Chapter Five

Philosophy of Art

The Search for a Definition of Art

What is Art? There are various ways of approaching this ancient question, one being to ask whether there is any prospect of giving a definition of "art" that is both succinct and informative. In an essay in *Philosphical Problems*[1] Papanoutsos takes up the question in this way.

In Papanoutsos's estimation Western philosophers, in trying to work out a definition of the term, have tended to classify art under one or another of five main headings. Some have regarded art as representation—of reality whether physical or historical or under some other aspect. Others have interpreted it as a form of play, a shedding of inhibition in a sheer freedom to create. It has been assimilated by some to dream experience, the suggestion again being that it affords a certain kind of release. It has been taken as a revelation, in sensory media, of the inmost essence of things. And it has been characterized as a fulfillment of man's need to bring about form and order, "significant" form as has often been said.

Papanoutsos finds these characterizations radically inadequate. In the case of the first two at any rate, there are art forms which obviously fall outside their scope. To try to characterize a Gothic church, a symphony, or a lyric poem as "representative" is simply inept. To regard as a form of play any work of art which it would be normal to consider motivated by "the spirit of seriousness," like a tragic drama or an El Greco painting, is grotesque. More generally: all five characterizations suffer from the fact that, even so far as they *can* apply to works of art, they do not say enough. They do not convey what kind of representation, diversion, etc., a work of art, as distinct from nonartistic objects or occupations or preoccupations, can purport to be. In other words, they fail to identify that essential criterion the presence or absence of which means that a thing has or has not artistic quality. Papanoutsos's line of argument is, in effect, that you cannot so elaborate the idea of representation, or of play, etc., as to have it capture the essence of art, or even of a specific kind of art. That something is "art" is not a function of its being representative, or recreative, or anything else which the five characterizations make it out to be. Nor, he affirms, is it a function of some or all of these properties taken in combination. However you combine them, the "hard core" of art, or in other terms, the specific differentiating factor, resists capture. In the immediate context[2] this is asserted rather as if it were intuitively obvious, but Papanoutsos proceeds so to depict what he takes to be the essentials of art that the five characterizations, whether taken singly or in combination, do appear to be peripheral at best.

"Art" in this context designates a human activity rather than the product of that activity; and for present purposes the term covers both the creative working of the artist and the "receptivity"[3] of those to whom, in one way or another, he addresses himself. It will not be surprising, therefore, if the essentials of art, so understood, cannot be conveyed in a neat formula. Papanoutsos himself professes to provide no such summary answer to the problem. His presentation of the matter is, instead, nonformal and, in a manner, indirect: not so much a collection of theses about art as a series of reminders that art "is what it is, and not another thing."[4] Art, he holds, is on a par with, and as autonomous as, those other great undertakings into which human beings characteristically enter in trying to come to terms with their "world," the religious, the theoretical, and the practical-moral; and as such it has its own irreducible scale of values. The beautiful may not be the object of a special sense, as some eighteenth-century thinkers were prepared to suggest, but along with certain other qualities it *is* the object of a special kind of experience, aesthetic experience, which Papanoutsos wishes to acknowledge and the nature of which he attempts to convey, albeit obliquely and by means of hints rather than definitive pronouncements. Such a degree of obliqueness may be inevitable. On his success or failure in "locating" and depicting aesthetic experience in his chosen manner, however, depends the effectiveness of his argument that the five characterizations of art with which we started do not get to the heart of the subject matter.

The topic is therefore crucial. This is how Papanoutsos writes about it in the essay being considered, the account being an outline which he strives to fill in elsewhere:

Aesthetic experience is a phenomenon which cannot be elucidated in terms of logic, but can only *be described*. We do not know it through concepts; we recognize it by living it. Its basis is emotive. As a developing process it reaches completion in a quite special *emotion* . . . which it is appropriate and convenient to call aesthetic. It is to be thought of as a state of well-being which involves not only sensory pleasure but also spiritual exaltation. It not only liberates the spiritual powers, but it brings them into harmony with one another and reconciles man with "himself." When it takes possession of us, we have the feeling that our life is being intensified and at the same time uplifted, that our inner world has gained both strength and nobility.[5]

If this general and (it must be confessed) somewhat lyrical depiction of aesthetic experience is acceptable, what it is describing is certainly something which the five characterizations fail to capture. But whether it is acceptable cannot at this stage be settled. The whole weight of the passage rests on a notion which is one of the most controversial in modern aesthetics, namely that of *aesthetic emotion*. If any part of the outline demands to be filled in, this one does. *Is* it "appropriate and convenient" to recognize and think in terms of such an emotion?

Papanoutsos gives full consideration to this question elsewhere, and his argument will be reviewed later in the present chapter. Here it is sufficient simply to indicate two features of the position which he holds. The first is that, as we might say, it is not psychologically "competitive"; that is, while it is not out of the question to envisage recognizing *aesthetic emotion* as a psychological concept, Papanoutsos does not attempt to prove its existence, as

one "emotion" among others, in terms of any particular psychological theory. His approach is phenomenological, rather, but
also such as "to make the psychologists think." What in fact he
tries to do is to show that the emotions which we experience as
being proper to aesthetic situations, whether the situations are
of a relatively simple kind or contrived and sophisticated, are
"of a different quality, weigh with us quite differently, in comparison with the common emotions of everyday life."[6] To take
a classic example: the pity and terror of which Aristotle speaks
as arising in the audience at a performance of a tragedy, and as
undergoing a certain catharsis in the process, are, or at any rate
become, emotions of "another kind, 'purified,' i.e. reflective
[*elloges*] and consonant with a high level of spiritual sensitivity."[7]
Clearly, there is much in this hint that needs, and is worth,
development.

The second feature of Papanoutsos's position is his insistence
that "aesthetic emotion" really does provide the specific differentiation which an attempt at a definition of "art," in any such
terms as those with which we began, needs if it is to say anything
to the point at all. "Without this purpose and this result [sc.
"of providing the sensitive and cultured person with a great and
unique good: aesthetic emotion"] 'imitation' is imitation, 'play'
play, a 'dream' a dream, an 'idea' an idea, and 'form' form—Art
they never become."[8] This does not mean, however, that a definition of "art" which provides for "aesthetic emotion" as having
the status just adumbrated is necessarily succinct and informative.
On the contrary, as the sequel will probably show, if it is succinct
it will not be informative (except to those who already take it
for granted), and if it is informative it will not be succinct. But
in any case, if Papanoutsos is right about the nature of aesthetic
experience and the status of aesthetic emotion, the effect of his
being so is to raise the question whether the five characterizations
are worth persevering with at all, as elements in a definition of
"art." In the passage just quoted, he writes as if art could be
imitation with a difference, play with a difference, an idea with
a difference, and so on. But since the difference makes all the
difference, it seems as if *it* should be the substance of any effective

definition; that *it* is what requires elucidation and expansion to let us realize in what way art "is what it is." The notions of imitation, play, and so on have become vestigial in the account, and should be allowed to drop out. At any rate that seems to be so if we profess to be examining art in general, and not to be highlighting what art *can* be in special circumstances, whether imitative, playful, formally significant, or anything else.

Realism, Idealism, and the Aesthetic

The question of aesthetic emotion will be taken up in the next section. In this one the concern is still with the general topic of aesthetic experience, but now as reached by Papanoutsos along another route, namely his dialectical discussion of the issue between aesthetic realism and aesthetic idealism.[9] Some of his most characteristic points of view are expressed or hinted at in this discussion.

It is part and parcel of Papanoutsos's dialectical style of thinking that its objective should be a "mean" between extremes. But a "mean" in this context is something that has to be worked at, or worked out: it is not there to be discovered in any rule-of-thumb fashion. Part of the reason for this is that, as Aristotle once observed, "to the mean in some cases the deficiency, in some the excess is more opposed."[10] In Papanoutsos's discussion of aesthetic realism and idealism it appears fairly clearly that, granted his efforts to do justice to the realist position, it is to realism that his "mean," or for present purposes his ultimate judgment of the status of aesthetic experience, is the more opposed.

What then is the nature of the polarity as Papanoutsos sees it? The classic slogan of extreme realism is that art is imitation *(mimesis)*, whether of Nature or of Life. It is in these that beauty ultimately resides; in these every aesthetically admirable object either resides or, if it is an artifact, has its "origin." The business of art, consequently, is always to strive to create the most faithful likeness of some feature of the natural or the human world. What the most perfect art produces may always be inferior to the beauty of Nature or of "Real Life" itself, but in all sorts of ways art helps us to "see" beauty and to share the excitement in the face of Nature or of Life which the artist himself has experienced.

So much for realism. The extreme contrary of this view is that Nature and Life in themselves are neither beautiful nor ugly. Not even the landscape painter or the portrait painter "copies" anything. His products are, rather, "visions, ideals which the artist's imagination has fashioned out of the whirl of inspiration."[11] Just as much as that of characters in literature, their being is "of the spirit."[12] This is the view of extreme idealism; and, like extreme realism, it manifests some rather obvious difficulties which Papanoutsos notes. Yet, although he claims that the truth is shared between the two theories, his own position (as already hinted) is highly sympathetic to idealism. An "art," he points out, which did nothing but "represent" reality, making accuracy its supreme virtue, might be of a wonderful dexterity, but would not be "of the spirit," which must be creative. The true artist takes possession of the world spiritually: he can be said to "realize" something within his work,[13] something which *forms* in effect a revelation of his own vision. "The man of literature is in the strict sense of the term a maker [*poietēs*]."[14] We may say, if we like, that certain works of art represent real objects; but it is where imitation ends and creation begins that the aesthetic dimension of such works is first apprehended. The beginnings of poetry, Papanoutsos remarks in another context, lie not in "the experience of life generally," but in "a *certain quality* which this experience acquires, when it is given form by or received into a consciousness which is functioning aesthetically."[15]

So: it is "not that Nature and Life *are,* but that they *become* beautiful (or ugly) at the hands of us ourselves. . . . Things or events take on aesthetic value within our perceptive capacity."[16] We quite ordinarily speak of "finding something beautiful," but this should be taken to mean that we "have been *able to form* an aesthetically satisfactory image of it within our perceptive capacity."[17] At the same time Papanoutsos does hold (and he elaborates this viewpoint throughout a detailed discussion of many art forms, notably schools of painting) that the artist has no absolute authority over the world of natural or humanistic objects.

On the contrary, he remarks, "the representations and myths of Art must persuade us";[18] and this is a pregnant saying. But it does not seriously modify the dominant emphasis, in this part of Papanoutsos's work, on artistic creativity, or the dominant interest in the *subject* (the practitioner or the experiencer) of artistic activity. It is no more than a "realistic" qualification to be borne in mind when we are considering his pervasive doctrine (to be discussed later) that aesthetic experience is one, and a very important, kind of human freedom.

In sketching these views the author has reproduced some phraseology which is characteristically Greek but not English. Talk of "taking possession of the world spiritually" and of "consciousness functioning aesthetically" is difficult to paraphrase in natural English idioms. For that matter, the general use of the terms "spirit" *(pneuma)* and "soul" *(psychē)* in reference to the focal area of aesthetic experience is expressive of a style which English writers would now be rather shy of using. (The difficulty which English translators have with the German *Geist* is comparable.) It would be unduly dismissive to say that these terms are just a manner of speaking—markers of some sort of dualism in human functioning, but not implying an old-fashioned two-substance theory of what man is. Their use is not as perfunctory as this makes it sound. The realm of "spirit" (as of "soul") is that in which man is, in a sense, master. It includes his efforts to assimilate, to get to know the world that he has to contend with, to make it his own with the means of perception and the modes of thinking, the categories and the theories that he develops. The realm is one in which he "functions" rather than "is a function of " anything.

Now this holds not only of his managing the world for his own purposes, through his understanding of it in all sorts of ways. The "spiritual" is wider than the investigative and the theoretical. Man has also a curious power of detachment, an ability to "see" the world in ways which involve no purposive interference with it. This, the aesthetic attitude, is another *autonomous* power. It is not a matter of restraint, of stopping short of doing something to the world or of forming theories about it.

We are able "to keep ourselves at a certain distance" from whatever we are concerned with aesthetically, as Papanoutsos remarks,[19] but there is no question of the aesthetic attitude's being, so to speak, an aborted part of the theoretical. As a way of "seeing" the world it is an achievement in its own right, something to be pursued for its own sake; as Papanoutsos also observes,[20] it actually debars the theoretical attitude, just as the theoretical debars it. Like the theoretical, however, it can demand all sorts of effort for its fulfillment. To say that consciousness "functions" aesthetically, then, is to say that it does something on its own, drawing upon resources and calling forth initiatives as complex in their way and as distinctive as those which are demanded by reason and the theoretical understanding. This activity is part of what makes an authentic human being. It represents a special kind of mastery over the world. And that it is an activity and not an undergoing is at least part of what is meant by assigning it to the realm of "spirit."

What, however, is it that consciousness "does on its own" when it is said to be "functioning aesthetically"? This question is difficult (perhaps impossible) to answer satisfactorily in general terms, with any degree of definition and in a sufficiently comprehensive way. Any attempt to define "the aesthetic," whether with reference to consciousness or to experience or to value, typically encounters the difficulty of making a transition from the negative features of what it is sought to define, to others. The same applies to statements *about* the aesthetic, which do not purport to be attempts at formal definition of the phrase; as, for example, the following: "Aesthetic value is not to be identified with serviceability, ease of use, convenience or comfort, but is connected with a property of another kind belonging to the object: with the entire form taken by the expression of some intention, with the perfect sensory rendering of a thought."[21]

To make the second part of this statement explicit and concrete instead of just schematic and suggestive requires the kind of serial examination of the varieties of aesthetic experience which Papanoutsos, in *Aesthetics*, in fact undertakes. He does not altogether eschew the attempt formally to elaborate such propositions, but his analyses are typically *in context,* and because of his repeated insistence on the "autonomy" of aesthetic experience they could not be expected anyhow to be definitive. The basic thing that has to be done in attempting a general exegis of "the aesthetic" is to help people see how it is located in experience, how it occurs vis-à-vis other forms of experience. Beyond that we must be content with pointers. "The aesthetic," Papanoutsos observes, "is not a continuation of the nonaesthetic (with a difference of coefficient in intensity and extent), nor is it a variation of it (with the qualitative differentiation of being purely intuitional and emotive), but it is a new functioning of our inner life. Aesthetic emotion occurs as a transmutation and transformation of others, as a new psychical state."[22]

About aesthetic emotion something will be said more directly to the point in the next section. At this stage, however, it would be helpful to look for some elucidation of the remark just quoted, that the aesthetic (meaning aesthetic experience) is "a new functioning of our inner life." It will be in the context of this "new functioning" that aesthetic emotion, assuming that the term does designate something distinctive, occurs. We may obtain some help from a discussion by Papanoutsos of what he calls "emotional nuances" of the experience of art.[23] These emotional nuances do not "add up to" a phenomenon to which the distinguishing title, "aesthetic emotion," may be applied; but they are, it would seem, to be interpreted as preconditions of such a phenomenon.

The first is a pleasure which we discover, whether in the creation or in the contemplation of art, in finding ourselves in a certain sense on the periphery of daily life, beyond its complications, difficulties, and gracelessness. The second, not wholly unconnected with the first, is a feeling of relief from the goadings of theoretical enquiry and the burden of coming to terms with the world conceptually, as also from practical necessities of all kinds. We occupy for the time being the position of a spectator, though not, most emphatically not, that of a totally uninvolved spectator. Papanoutsos applies to these two nuances the engaging label, "pleasure of parenthesis"; but he remarks that what they amount to is something essentially negative. The remaining nuances are more positive.

The third is enchantment with the fictive character of much art, imaginative, perhaps dreamlike, perhaps mystic; art that exemplifies the graphic and the exotic to which we may readily give ourselves over. The fourth is a feeling of fulfillment; art provides both enrichment and refinement in the quality of our experience of life. Fifth, there is a delight in form, in perfection of rhythm, composition, physical shape, and so on. Last, there is the experience of "having one's eyes opened" to a new vision or apprehension of the world with which an original work of art may provide us.

The list of such "nuances" could perhaps be extended, but it is their nature rather than their number that matters for present purposes. What they suggest is that the experience of art is something very much on its own, more or less elaborately "managed" and in conspicuous ways *not* continuous with either the routines or the chances and contingencies of "ordinary" experience. A "new functioning of our inner life" has been *contrived,* emotionally "colored" in the way just described. In the course of that functioning there may occur in us further emotions, specific emotions having some affinity with those of "ordinary" experience. But because of that functioning emotions are apt to occur in a new way, with less turmoil, more "purely" than in everyday life, more reflectively. The author will try to make sense of this suggestion in the next section.

Aesthetic Emotion

It is clear from the last section that the "autonomy" which Papanoutsos would ascribe to the aesthetic in general he would ascribe in some particular fashion to aesthetic emotion. The question whether there is a distinctive aesthetic emotion, and if so what are its criteria, is much in dispute in modern philosophy. Obviously it offers a challenge to reductionists, whether to those who would reduce aesthetic emotion to one or another (not necessarily the same one in each instance) of various "commonplace" emotions (like joy, fear, anguish, sadness, or wonderment), or to those who would have it equivalent to a complex of these. Papanoutsos examines a representative selection of such attempts and rejects them, in a common-sense style, on the grounds that they do less than justice to plain experience, in this case aesthetic experience unprejudiced by theory. And, like Burke, he would hold in effect that if, for example, you go to a theatrical performance simply in order to experience some emotion, say fascinated horror, in a high degree, then the chances are that you would do better to betake yourself to the life of the streets and marketplaces outside. On the other hand, it is not Papanoutsos's view that there is one distinctive, unvaried emotion, which we may call "aesthetic emotion" and which it is at least part of the object of our aesthetic undertakings that we should experience. In discussing poetry he remarks that poetry *idealizes* emotion, transmits emotion to us in idealized form. "The fear or wonder which is expressed poetically, which is communicated in a poetic experience, is no longer the 'common' fear or the 'common' wonder, but an 'other' fear, an 'other' wonder."[24] This certainly does not mean that our emotion is merely "phenomenal" (corresponding to an hallucination or an illusion): such a suggestion would be inept. "In this situation we do genuinely feel fear or wonder. But the content of the emotion has here been changed in nature— meaning that it has become something universal, schematic, of an ideal purity."[25] It is the "pure quality"[26] of fear, of wonder and the rest, that poetry thus conveys to us.

It may seem as if Papanoutsos is having to maintain a fairly delicate balance in order to keep away from reductionism without having recourse to the basically implausible idea of a standard "aesthetic emotion," on its own. A down-to-earth critic might ask what is to differentiate these "idealized" fears, wonderments, and so on from being merely watered-down occurrences of the fears, wonderments, and so on to which we are exposed when outside the contrived setting of the theater, the art gallery, or the concert hall, as the case may be. *Is* not Papanoutsos liable to the predicament noted by Burke?

To begin to answer this question it is helpful to refer to Papanoutsos's thinking about Aristotle. Aristotle's views, in the

Poetics, about tragedy have had a deep influence on Papanoutsos's attitude, not only to the aesthetic emotions which come into question particularly in that context, but to art as a whole.[27] Briefly, this is how Papanoutsos interprets Aristotle:

Tragedy with its pity and fear, its task being to "prepare" [these and other passions] and to interweave [them] with the lofty moral and religious attitudes of "love of humanity," *purifies passions of this kind* and consequently brings the soul to experience not common pity and fear, i.e., passions without deeper significance, unmixed with reason and subject to no control, which are often found in conflict with one another and which with their immoderateness disrupt the internal harmony of the soul, but a *purified* pity and fear, sentiments which arise from the capturing of a deeper moral and religious signification. These sentiments are emotions *of another quality,* passions imbued with reason, "moderated," in harmony among themselves and with the rest of the spiritual "world."[28]

If this interpretation of aesthetic emotion, in association with the Aristotelian catharsis, is correct it has great significance, according to Papanoutsos, for it provides us with one way of looking, not just at tragedy, but at art in general. He himself believes that it is both correct as an interpretation and acceptable on its merits. He is therefore prepared to say that all art "purifies" in the way in which for Aristotle tragic art purifies.

The "moderation" of passion to which he gives emphasis in the passage just quoted is the key to this extension. Using a slightly different terminology one might suggest that in everyday experience the emotions are often prereflective. They occur, more or less strongly, in connection with experiences which, so to speak, give us no chance with them. An opening in a game provides us with hope; an act of cruelty makes us angry; someone's illness engenders anxiety; and so on. In no such case is the perspective adopted one of seeing the emotion in context. Aesthetically, however, the perspective that we are adopting is invariably of that kind. Here the emotions are, in a fashion, reflective: what we are absorbed in is such and such a dramatic, pictorial, musical, architectural, etc., context as productive of this or that emotion, and the emotion as reflective of that context. The emotion is "moderated," to return to Papanoutsos's term, as being itself *of interest,* because it is reflective of the situation in question. From this point of view, art is a controlled exploration of the emotional qualities of things and situations; but not, of course, any kind of controlled explanation—what kind it is, is another matter. Thus far, then—and it is a long way—Papanoutsos is prepared to take the Aristotelian notion of catharsis. Summarily, he holds that art can be characterized as "purification,"[29] this term having the significance of "enrichment and lustration, the intensification and the elevation of our emotional life."[30]

The paraphrase just given will not, it is to be hoped, suggest that Papanoutsos is open to the charge of intellectualizing emotion. That is not what "purification," or any of its partial equivalents, means. But can he now be seen to have escaped the criticism that his "aesthetic" emotions are but watered-down versions of the "common" ones? Papanoutsos answers this question with a concession and a counterattack, the latter taking him to another position of significance. Perhaps, he concedes, the emotions in question are from one point of view "poorer" than their everyday counterparts. From another point of view, however—and now a point already made can be explained—they are "richer." The fear, for example, with which we are inspired by *Antigone* or *King Lear* may be said to contain the elements of "ordinary" fear, but also to transcend them. "It is as if the [artisitic] form which expresses it gives us an authority over it."[31]

This saying may help to bring out part of the significance of the notion of "reflection," already discussed. But it also marks out another position which Papanoutsos wishes to occupy, namely that aesthetic experience represents a distinctive kind of human freedom. In the present context, this kind of freedom appears both as a liberation from emotion in one regard and as a control over emotion in another.

Papanoutsos does not wish to imply for his distinction, between aesthetic and other emotion, greater sharpness *in application* than it actually has. He remarks that as a matter of psychological fact it is impossible to draw clear dividing-lines between common-

place and aesthetic responses and the corresponding emotions.[32]
(This is surely an overstatement.) He notes also that in the case
of tragedy it is not easy to draw boundaries between aesthetic
emotion on the one hand and moral admiration and religious awe
on the other. The category of "the sublime" in general provides
difficulty for the phenomenology of such matters. Tragedy, however, presents a further problem which is not just a question of
distinguishing between emotions, "everyday" and "aesthetic,"
that are, in a manner of speaking, counterparts. A certain reconciliation of opposites also appears here, and it has to be made
intelligible. Papanoutsos's explanation of this does something
further to fill out the notions of "enrichment" and "exaltation,"
which have already appeared as part of the more definitional side
of his account of tragedy. The problem is that tragedy, while it
oppresses us, also "exalts us over ourselves," as he says engagingly.[33]

The Tragic, for all the spiritual perturbation which it causes our sensibility, delights us with its deep human significance—*it strains and
brings into tumult . . . but at the same time uplifts our emotional life.* This
uplifting of soul transforms the sense of affliction (the offshoot of sympathy) into aesthetic joy. Not, that is, into common pleasure . . . but
into an emotion which can retain its bitter tone and yet delight us,
because it satisfies our spiritual nature. In face of the Tragic . . .
psychophysiological man is grieved, but the spiritual man within us
exults. Affliction . . . has a greatness of its own: it adorns and softens
the character of the guilty man himself.[34]

Aesthetic Experience as a Form of Freedom

In his account of the transformational power of tragedy Papanoutsos touches more than once, and in different ways, on
what, it may be suggested, are the leading ideas of his *Aesthetics,*
namely that aesthetic experience is an achievement rather than
an undergoing, and that the achievement is one of human freedom
in a basic "spiritual" sense. In this respect, tragedy is a paradigm
of what Papanoutsos would say about all art. The freedom involved may be looked at in a variety of interconnected ways.
There is the freedom of emotional liberation and that of emotional
mastery or control. There is freedom in the harmony of those

powers which we exercise in our "aesthetic functioning." The creativity of the artist is freedom in the highest degree; and in achieving this freedom he may be followed at least part of the way by those who read, see, or hear his work with insight. In connection with creativity mention is often made of a spiritual transformation of reality, achieved through the artistic fusion of form and content: here perhaps is to be found the essential condition of the freedom which the artist exercises. About certain of these aspects of freedom more can appropriately be said than has been said or hinted at already.

The idea of freedom as harmony is one which seems intuitively acceptable, but very difficult to redeem from vagueness. Aesthetic pleasure, Papanoutsos says, is yielded by living through a phase of intense and harmonious inner life, in circumstances where "the spiritual powers converge unforcedly to coordinate their operation."[35] The convergence is that which brings about the qualitative emotional change discussed already in terms of "purification"; but still one has to grope in order to discover just what it is that converges. Perhaps the clue is that art is a kind of resolution or reconciliation of attitudes on a certain ideal level; the handling of naturally divergent, recalcitrant or dissonant material which ordinarily would affect us "in all sorts of ways," but which a disciplined imagination can enable us to "make something of "; as, for example, the imagination of the sculptor can take form in what was originally obdurate, unfashioned marble, or that of the playwright in the "dramatic" resolution of situations in which human passions, ambitions, loves, hatreds, and so on would "naturally" run an untidy and, in a way, formless course.

Obscure as this suggestion may sound, it perhaps puts us on the track of what Papanoutsos means when he speaks, with reference to artistic activity, of *"the struggles and strivings of properly conscious life* [sc. as distinct from subconscious life], which create out of turbid psychical material, namely the yearnings and longings of a sensitive human being, the brilliant symbolic world of the artistic masterpiece, and its beauty. . . ."[36] The issue of this contest, he insists, is the refinement and elevation of the emotions, and its endpoint is spiritual freedom.[37] It would cer-

tainly seem that the "unforcedness" which he ascribes to the
convergence and coordination of powers achieved in aesthetic
experience is a peace which descends on them, and not at all a
characteristic of the artistic enterprise as it progresses. The harmony attained, however, can thus be regarded also as a freedom
attained, the freedom from being affected in this manner or that,
from being emotionally "taken" by some situation in no coherent
way, and from an associated inability to "see" the form of what
confronts us. To achieve all this is spiritual liberation, and also
mastery or control. It may seem natural, though, to suggest next
that more is involved in the attainment of artistic freedom than
just control, *just* the imposition of order upon disarray. We have
to do with the "creation" of order out of disarray: hence we should
look now at what Papanoutsos has to say abour artistic freedom
as creativity.

A conspicuous example of artistic creativity is that of lyric
poetry, which, as Papanoutsos notes, is as far removed as can be
from the practice of art as "imitation." The lyric poet indeed
exercises a "cosmogonic power." "He creates, 'manufactures' a
spiritual situation with his words."[38] But we do not have to
depend on such a conspicuously nonmimetic activity as that of
the lyric poet in order to convey the nature of artistic creativity
(and capture its feeling of freedom). Even the landscape painter,
as previously remarked, is no "copier" of reality. "In nature there
are no expressive lines, evocative colors, surfaces and masses throb-
bing with feeling, light which hushes and shadows which
speak."[39] These are not objective elements, there to be differentiated and depicted. Rather, they are "forms which the artist's
vision imposes on objects, creations beyond the actual of the
artistic consciousness."[40]

Speaking in these terms, Papanoutsos seems clearly to be in
sympathy with an idealistic stance. At the same time (and here
an element of aesthetic realism reasserts itself in Papanoutsos's
thinking) an artist's freedom in this "creative" respect is not of
an utterly arbitrary kind. As he says, strikingly, "Art is a transcendence, not a violation of reality,"[41] and "in Art the object

is taken possession of spiritually, not set at naught: it preserves its rights."[42]

Such sayings as these are not mere obiter dicta, because Papanoutsos in fact makes a great deal of the thought behind them. The idealist tone is maintained when he reminds us that nature and life do not "have," but take on aesthetic value from the (creative) artistic consciousness. Yet we have to recognize a certain reciprocity of dependence in the relationship between aesthetic subject and aesthetic object. "In the achievements of Art, Nature reveals and discovers man just as man does Nature."[43] In other words, the artistic presentation of nature and of life must, to a significant degree, be an assimilation. Rights are retained. . . . And artistic freedom is thus put in context: the artist creates beauty, but the creation is not ex nihilo. "Beauty from one point of view is the bringing into brotherhood of necessity and freedom, of the causal properties of things and the intentionality of ideas, of world and man."[44] So we reach the point that art has its "object," presents a "reality," but the reality so presented must be (and the phrase is used repeatedly) a "spiritual transmutation."[45] This transmutation, Papanoutsos suggests, is seen most conspicuously in music.[46]

It is open to question whether Papanoutsos is not being *over*-accommodating to realism at this point. The notion of an artistic "object" is unsatisfactory anyhow, being ambiguous as between something represented (or, on the extreme view, imitated or copied) and such actual material as the physical or the psychical world may make available for the artist's purposes. But this is a secondary difficulty. It is more important to remark that the "reality" to which in some way the artistic product must be faithful stands very differently vis-à-vis different forms of art. For example, the *hubris* which is punished in a Greek tragedy is an accentuation of normal human arrogance; but it is intelligible as such, and one *may* think of normal human arrogance as the raw material out of which *hubris* is constructed by the artistic imagination. Also, one can see that this "reality" may exert certain controls over what that imagination aspires to. But is there anything like this contrast, is the contrast there to be made, in (let us say) symphonic music? On the one hand there are, unquestionably, the sounds and sound patterns of nature, and on the other musical assonance and rhythm. But to think of the former as being any kind of raw material for the latter seems far-fetched; still more so to think of it as being a "realistic" constraint upon what the composer may dare.

The suggestion is not that the notion of "spiritual transmutation" is an inept one; far from it. What is uncertain is how generally it is applicable through the various forms of artistic creativity. Papanoutsos himself does certainly hold that it makes sense to think of the musical consciousness as transmuting spiritually "the myriad-voiced and unorganized reality of the natural world of sound."[47] And yet, significantly, he points out that music has a great advantage over all other arts, in that it is "free of the tyranny of the 'object'—whether this is some 'thing,' as in painting or sculpture, or 'happening,' as in poetry or drama."[48] The subject-object dialectic, effectively used by Papanoutsos over great sweeps of his subject, nevertheless works unequally well in application to the different forms of art.

This leaves unaffected, however, the importance of *freedom* as a unifying idea running through Papanoutsos's account of aesthetic experience and of the arts. It is worth remarking that the freedom which he makes thus central is not the prerogative of a relatively select few, the artists among us. For one thing, as Papanoutsos well recognizes, we most of us have something of the artist in us. But in any case, even if we think of the reader, hearer, or spectator as standing in opposition to the artist, so to speak, it is still possible to recognize a freedom which, in one of these capacities, we may achieve. The notion of "freedom" as a function of understanding is an old one, inside and outside of philosophy. Papanoutsos here introduces it as a function of aesthetic "understanding." He explains this as the interpretation of a work (though not an arbitrary interpretation) through and by means of our own experience of life. The work has to be "refashioned" within our own consciousness and its "expressive forms" filled out with thought, feeling, awareness, etc., which are *ours* as the upshot of our individual experiences. Without such activity "we cannot be receptive of its redemptive charm."[49] So, as spectators, hearers, or readers we are not related to the work passively. The work does not "belong to us" as it "belongs to" the artist who created it, and yet there is a sense in which it may become as much ours as his. Think in this connection of the actor in relation to the playwright.

If "interpretation" means in the last resort re-creation of the work through personal inspiration, and consequently if the interpreter par excellence is the actor who gives himself body and soul to the performance of a drama, we can say that in the depths of every reader, spectator or hearer of a work of art there is to a greater or lesser extent an "actor" who "plays."[50]

In other words, we all have something of the actor's creative freedom.

"Greatness" in Art

Can works of art be put into any sort of hierarchy, in which one can be accorded greater artistic value than another?[51] The answer is, of course, yes and no. There are many points of view from which different works of art can be compared, and as many possible answers, affirmative or negative, to the question. There are other points of view according to which the very idea of comparison seems nonsense. The judges who select paintings or sculptural works for the annual exhibition of an Academy or Art Society will often enough have fairly firm ideas as to what is acceptable and what not; some might conceivably go so far as to commit themselves to an approximate even if not exhaustive individual order of merit. Within a particular art form one may certainly succeed to this extent in comparing one work with another evaluatively, although the feasibility of comparison recedes according as one is confronted, in that art form, with a diversity of general styles, schools, epochs, artistic materials, and so on. When, however, one entertains the idea of comparing, say, a piece of Ming porcelain to a symphonic poem, can the idea be put into effect at all? Can one indulge in comparisons here on any serious basis, without (that is) taking frivolous, perhaps even vacuous, criteria as one's professed standard?

If what we have in mind in this instance is the "beauty"[52] of the two items in question, then comparison seems pointless. Beauty is a perfection, a certain mark of success in a specific artistic endeavor. So regarded, it is not subject to any common measure, not at any rate when what we have to deal with are items *as* specific in their way as a piece of porcelain and a piece of music. This is Papanoutsos's view, which he shares with a considerable company of other aestheticians; for example he quotes approvingly a somewhat macabre apophthegm of Etienne Souriau: "It is with pure beauty as it is with death; all that partakes of it is on the same level."[53] So much, then, for the attempt to compare these and the like disparate objects in point of *beauty*.

Yet there are other ways of comparing thoroughly disparate artistic objects, which, for all that the principles on which they proceed are difficult, perhaps very difficult, to formulate, have been traditionally recognized and can yield assessments of striking unanimity at various levels of professionalism. *Significance, stature, sublimity:* these three terms of reference, which Papanoutsos now brings into the reckoning, are representative of a category of assessment which can undoubtedly be used to set individual works apart, as being of a certain supreme value not only among other works of their general kind, but among works of any artistic kind. There is *some* way in which the Parthenon has value transcending that of a Sèvres vase; the *St. Matthew Passion,* that of a fine tapestry; or the *Divine Comedy,* that of an elegant piece of choreography—to say nothing of the monumentality of each of these works as compared with other examples "of their own kind"—of ceremonial architecture, or musical or poetic composition, as the case may be. Whatever the criteria on which such comparisons depend, it seems safe to suggest that they are neither frivolous nor vacuous. The comparisons do seem to make sense in that they are a way of registering the sheer "greatness" of certain achievements. Perhaps "it goes without saying" that the Parthenon transcends a piece of "fine art" in value: but where the remark may seem otiose, that is because it makes so much sense as to be obvious!

These general reflections, however, conceal a general and most notorious problem—whether in speaking, for example, of the "transcendent value" of some celebrated work of art we are not stepping outside the bounds of strictly aesthetic evaluation. If such a work has something out of the ordinary to say to us (as we might put it), is that "something" necessarily aesthetic, as distinct from moral or perhaps religious? Is there a level of judgment at which there can be a fusion of aesthetic and moral or religious values—or refusion (as perhaps we should say, in that we have come dialectically a long way from the supposed primitive level at which these values have not yet been culturally sorted out)? The very suggestion will appear shocking in the light of all the earnest work which has gone on, in modern aesthetics, guided by the maxim that speaking from an aesthetic point of view *means,* at least in part, *not* speaking from a moral or from a religious or from a variety of other points of view.[54]

Yet the suggestion is one which Papanoutsos may be taken seriously to be offering, and it is one which merits serious consideration. Not all conflation is confusion, particularly where the conflation is considered and deliberate. In this instance he takes up the question, to what sort of value works of art are susceptible, in the form of a general antinomy which we often enough come up against in considering the relations between art and morality. On the one hand we tend to treat as a veritable "axiom"[55] the principle that the criteria of aesthetic value are one thing, the measures of good and evil another. The objectives of art are simply not to be identified with the requirements of moral guidance. These propositions, indeed, are philosophically commonplace. What is not so commonplace is the other side of the matter, put by Papanoutsos in these terms:

Complete beauty, whether we think of it as attained in epic and dramatic poetry, or as in painting or sculpture, music or architecture, has about it an unmistakable moral greatness. We are made to feel, and to feel strongly, of artistic perfection that it involves more than just "persuading" our sensibility or simply bringing us inward delight; it leads to something different and much greater, bringing us to a state of ecstasy, engendering in us a sentiment become moral or religious in nature: namely awe and wonderment.[56]

This statement has just been called "the other side of the matter," and so Papanoutsos initially presents it as being. But, arguably, it is already more the *solution* of the antinomy than the representation of one of its two conflicting aspects. These aspects have got to be on the same level as one another, a level which we have got to get beyond if we wish to hold the two together satisfactorily in some "further" understanding of them. The antinomy, it may seem, is already latent in the first side of the matter, noted above. It lies properly, that is, in the tension which subsists between the basic aesthetic characteristics of a work, amounting to "beauty" in the sense originally noted in this section (or to some other overall "aesthetic" feature on that level), and the moral or religious characteristics which the work may possess, and manifest more or less powerfully but from an autonomous point of view. The tension is antinomic because the two points of view concerned are not just autonomous but exclusive of one another. This, certainly, is how they present themselves on a primary phenomenological analysis.

How much the ordinary man cares for the scrupulosity and puritanism of such analysis is, however, another matter. It is not unusual to experience a craving to rise above the level at which the strictly aesthetic and the strictly moral maintain their credentials; where the aesthetic and the moral rebarbatively keep their distance from one another. It may be that what Pananoutsos is doing in the passage quoted above is to give literate expression to this craving, and that there is something of a lacuna (the nature of which has been hinted at, correctly or incorrectly) in his representation of the whole situation as antinomic. For the explanation which he next proceeds to offer as "the solution of this antinomy"[57] is in effect an expansion of what he has already said on one side of the account.

It depends entirely upon recognizing a stratum of spiritual existence in which certain special modes of human experience—broadly, the theoretical, the moral, the aesthetic, and (presumably we should add) the religious—are separated out by philosophical analysis, and, of course, regarded also by common experience, for many purposes, as being autonomous functionings. As remarked already, we *can* think of such a stratum as a preanalytical and unsophisticated matrix from which certain kinds of differentiated human experience have yet to emerge. But— such seems to be Papanoutsos's idea—we can think of it also as a unity regained, through the mediation of differentiated human experience and where the experience is of such quality that it cannot, so to speak, contain itself but must spill over into other kinds. "This [inner] bond of unity is most clearly apparent in those outstanding creative achievements of the human spirit, in which theoretical thinking becomes responsible action and beauty takes on the sheen of morality."[58] Papanoutsos hastens to explain, however, that by "morality" in this context he means no sort of codified, established system of morals, but a fundamentally personal human attitude, of responsibility, care, and concern about what one is doing, which can endow some works of art with a "spiritual substantiality"[59] that others simply lack. "It is only with this sort of 'good' that the 'beautiful' can share exisence in the supreme achievements of Art."[60]

Otherwise put, such achievements have particular "*human* significance"—and in elaborating this idea Papanoutsos returns to the subject of the comparability of works of art. Of "human significance" he says:

It is a significance which admits of gradations, and on this account we do not simply put all worthy works of art into the same box—some we esteem and love more, some less. A painting or a piece of sculpture is not *more beautiful* than a vase or a rug fashioned with genuine and accomplished artistry, but *more significant;* likewise an architectural monument or a symphony is not *more beautiful* than a choice piece of ornamentation or an admirable choreographic pattern, but *more significant.* Among the various forms of art, regarded from a purely aesthetic point of view, no hierarchy can be entertained: beautiful works, to whatever artistic sector they belong, are equally beautiful. Not all arts, however, and not all worthy examples belonging to each particular art, have the same human depth, the same significance for our inner

life. . . . It is their degree of significance, and nothing else, that
constitutes their sublimity or greatness.[61]

The question now arises, inevitably, how we are to identify
and elucidate the criteria of *significance*. In considering this question, Papanoutsos is very chary of aiming at misplaced precision.
There is an inavoidable relativity in the notion of significance
even in the more "classic" realms of art: it cannot be made
completely objective. Works of art come to be regarded as "significant" within a cultural context that may be relatively general
and of great duration; the practice of a style of thought, more
or less widely held expectations as to the possibilities and the
limits of human achievement, the common recognition of spheres
of human activity that matter, and a corresponding universality
of feeling with regard to them—and so on. None of these can
be thought of as eternally given features, essential aspects of the
human situation.

In trying to convey what the "significance" of works of art
depends upon, the best we can do, Papanoutsos seems to suggest,
is to outline how such features as those just mentioned have
preoccupied or do preoccupy humanity, and how such preoccupation wells up from time to time in "great" works of art. We
may think, for example, of devotion to Nature or of man's im-
pelling interest in love and the erotic; on a different level, perhaps,
of dedication to the social (on the one hand) and of the cult of
individuality (on the other); of metaphysical anguish and yearning; and so on. In some features we recognize, but without
identifying for all time, what artistic significance, or "greatness,"
grows out of. The point is that at this level of reckoning we are
involved with something deeper than either mere "beauty" or
mere "moral rectitude." Herein consists Papanoutsos's attempt
to show that man is endowed with a greater spirituality than
finds expression in either the aesthetic or the ethical, on its own.

Chapter Six

The Temporal
and the Eternal

Science and History

The catholicity of Papanoutsos's interests in philosophy would not be conveyed completely without some reference to his philosophy of history. Toward the end of *Gnosiology*[1] Papanoutsos completes his survey of human knowledge by taking in two great areas, namely history and philosophy, between which and the mathematicoscientific there might seem to be fairly obvious discontinuity. In the course of the "gnosiological" discussions with which we have been concerned previously, Papanoutsos does, of course, have things to say about philosophy as a subject, or as a dimension of human thought; but in the main he is doing philosophy rather than talking about it. He now proceeds to look at history and philosophy as subjects; and for this purpose the general tenor of his discussion is to consider the two of them, successively, in their relationship to science. Are they continuous or homogeneous with science, the knowledge of nature, or rather the reverse? This section will be confined to his argument about history.

Taking up the comparison of history with science, first of all in a rather abstract way, Papanoutsos claims that the same logical structure is characteristic of the general method of each. That is: whether it is truths of history or truths about nature which are in question, they are tested and confirmed by the same criteria. On the side of content, each discipline acknowledges the need to achieve a continuously more objective basis; on that of form, a continuously more perfect organization. (The general theme

119

represented here will be familiar to the reader from the earlier discussions referred to above.) But this itself is a very *formal* observation. How does it work out, granted the manifest and immediate difference in subject matter which strikes one when one opens a work of history on the one hand, and consults a textbook of physics on the other? Is it not that historical argument moves characteristically from particulars to particulars, no doubt via general knowledge of one sort or another; and that a physical theory is characteristically an argument from one set of general positions to another set of general positions, via, of course, the particular observations and experiments that enable the second set of general positions to be occupied and held with tolerable security? The parts played by "the general" in the two modes of investigation are so different that to compare the two in point of objectivity and organization would seem not to take us very far at all.

Papanoutsos himself is not impressed by this way of looking at the matter. The considerations involved in it may be acceptable individually, but their bearing on one another and the general emphasis which they convey are questionable. "The view that the scope of its [sc. historical] researches is the particular, in contrast to science properly speaking, whose object of pursuit is exclusively the general, is not correct. The only distinction admissible in such terms between knowledge of nature and historical knowledge is that the first studies the particular in order to come to an understanding of the general, while the second seeks after the general in order to understand the particular. . . . Both rise to the plane of generality. . . ."[2]

Well, they do; and there are historical laws. Papanoutsos gives some examples of them. "A civilized community disintegrates either through the corrosion of internal social upheavals or through attacks by powerful neighbors. . . ." "When the demographic problem in a certain area becomes acute because of an increased birth-rate along with economic recession, serious political crises set in."[3] And so on. Leaving aside the question how "lawlike" these principles really are, one cannot but observe that they are relatively vague as well as general. To arrive at general historical truths that were less vague, one would probably have to make a compensating sacrifice of "law-likeness." It is to be doubted if such a situation obtains in natural science, where both generality of various levels and precision can be attained.

Also, it is part of the function of natural scientific laws to enable us to predict what will happen in specifiable future circumstances. Are historical "laws" such as to lend themselves to analogous purposes? Papanoutsos remarks that with the aid of such laws as have been mentioned the historian simply cannot anticipate beyond all refutation what will happen in such and such special circumstances to which, you might think, they will apply. Yet Papanoutsos will not take this and related factors as a defeat for his assimilative view; his insistence, that is, on the gnosiological affinity in important respects of natural science and history. For one thing, he thinks, doubts and hesitations of the kind just suggested reflect too partial a view of physics, regarded as the keystone science with which history is to be compared. The rigid necessitarian lawlike structure, which we tend submissively to attribute to its subject matter, belongs at best to the physics of the macrocosm; but elsewhere in physical science it has long since been abandoned in the revolutionary researches and theorizings of our contemporaries or near-contemporaries. So, the historian's inability to anticipate the future irrefutably is due, Papanoutsos is able to say boldly, to a feature which historical laws actually share with the most fundamental, statistically structured laws of physics, namely that they are laws "of large numbers" which will not necessarily cover the individual constituent a's, b's, etc., of future complexes.[4]

Granted this feature of them, however, Papanoutsos does regard historical laws as forward-looking, as providing *some* basis for the prediction and assessment of what is to happen. But it is possible to suggest a more austere view of them according to which they are strictly backward-looking; are, that is, the most carefully formulated and best-supported general records which we can assemble of what human beings have been and have done in such and such kinds of circumstance. The historian's business with such records, it may be suggested, is limited to their formulation and to their possible review in the light of the continuously extending past. Others may use them for predictive purposes, but in so using them they are behaving as social psychologists or as anthropologists, and not as historians. It is commonplace to speak of "the lessons of history," of course, and possibly the historian is better qualified to learn and apply them than anyone else. But is it in his capacity as *historian* that he does so?

Papanoutsos does not discuss this question explicitly, but he would probably wish to answer it in the affirmative. The question may seem persnickety: does it matter in what professional capacity one learns and applies the lessons of history? Perhaps not. But the question is of interest because it has a bearing on the "assimilative" side of Papanoutsos's writing about history and natural science. If prediction is part of the proper function of the historian qua historian, then history *is* more like natural science than it might otherwise seem to be. But again if so, this is perhaps to attribute to the world's historical knowledge a store of "laws" having a dependability, variety, and adaptability such as most professional historians would hesitate to claim for their subject over most of its scope. And perhaps this deficiency, if deficiency it be, is chronic.

As noted, Papanoutsos ascribes to the general method of history a determination to work toward a continuously more objective basis. Such a process, we are to take it, would be possible despite the fact that all history, in the nature of things, is written from a point of view, one which may or may not be peculiar to the individual historian. What offsets this is that historians do communicate, that there is a world of historical scholarship in which comment on and criticism of other historians' work is the norm; and where there can at least be correction and supplementation of work in which subjectivity merges into bias or untruth. It is, of course, only a "more objective" and not an "objective" basis which can thus be achieved. That said, it seems perhaps odd that Papanoutsos should go on next to emphasize the quintessential subjectivity of history, to stress not so much that history is unable to be other than subjective, as the rightness and propriety of its being subjective.[5] How does this emphasis square with progress toward objectivity?

It is fair to suggest that, although he does not bring out the difference quite explicitly, Papanoutsos has in mind two sorts of subjectivity, the one a tendency to narrowness of view, partiality, or prejudice, the other a bringing to bear of the *special* resources of mind, the understanding and the large sympathies which a historiographer may be fortunate enough to possess. The first sort must be overcome, and the overcoming we recognize as progress toward objectivity. The second sort, far from encouraging a blinkered approach, illuminates through the resourcefulness and value of *that* point of view; it liberalizes, not restricts; and it is this which enables history to be recognized (whatever be its affinities with natural science) as a "humane study." It can only be the second kind of subjectivity that Papanoutsos has in mind in the following passage, one which gives us another glimpse of his own humanism, and with which this (very selective) account of his views on history may appropriately be concluded:

Every "philosophically rounded" historical work (and to be "philosophically rounded" means in the present context that it has achieved completion both as a general survey of the subject and as a weighing of its elements) contains (manifestly or between the lines) and makes good a certain theoretical and moral capital. This capital is generally the product of personal achievement, an issue from and warrant of an internal world, a concrete human individuality. Of necessity, therefore, there is to be found at the very heart of historical truth, strong and ineffaceable, the element of subjectivity.[6]

Science and Philosophy

In his comparison of philosophy with science, as in that of history with science, Papanoutsos is more impressed by the affinities that are involved than by points of contrast. Against William James, he insists that there is no *gnosiological* distinction between science and critical philosophy. "Their respective truths," he says, "belong to the same genus. If the ideas pertaining to these two systems have not yet been brought into harmony within a construction of some higher form, this is a provisional state of affairs. . . ."[7] More expansively, he writes:

The distinction between science and philosophy, understood as signifying that we have to do with two essentially different courses taken
by theoretical reason, is an error. It is unjustified historically and
unfounded logically. . . . Logically there is no [sc. absolute] distinction between philosophy and science. Since in both cases the aim is the
theoretical grasping of reality, the discovery of truth; and since neither
the one nor the other is subject to any [sc. arbitrary] authority, but
both submit their findings to strict and objective testing, how can there
be a [sc. final] difference in the concepts expressive of them? The view
that to philosophy there belong those exalted and difficult subject
matters which science cannot or will not investigate, since it has at its
disposal neither method nor means of achieving any certainty with
regard to them; as also the view that, forced by the nature of its
problems to have recourse to inspiration and imagination rather than
observation and judgment, philosophy is closer to poetry than to science
. . . are neither correct nor in tune with present-day sentiment and
experience.[8]

Taken on its own, this passage may seem rather schematic and general. But the point to emerge is that philosophy is concerned in the last resort with reality (in its general aspects) and not exclusively with systems of expression; philosophy, that is to say, extends beyond logic—whether "formal" or "informal"—and is justified in setting itself at *truth* and not only at logical validity.

Whether the last word about the relationship between philos-
ophy and science is, in some such terms, an assimilative one or not, is of course open to argument. It may be felt that the likeness which Papanoutsos adduces is so general as to be unstriking, and that a certain unlikeness is both more dramatic and irremovable. For there is a difference in "order" between philosophy and science which Papanoutsos in *Gnosiology* tends to underplay, until a very late stage at which he does bring it out—but enigmatically.[9] (Note will be taken of that particular discussion in a moment.) It may be argued that philosophy *ab initio* undertakes a critical comparison of ways of describing or interpreting reality (and looks toward *truth* as the end of its critical survey of these ways); whereas

theoretical science, in any critical examination to which it may subject some scientific method, and even in a possible comparison of this method with some other, is interested principally in the development of the method as a definite method of reckoning or of expressing truths within a particular field of investigation; a field, that is, which, while not firmly closed off, constitutes nevertheless a relatively well-recognized and *to some extent* circumscribed area. In other words, theoretical science has a more vested interest in some particular method, as being an *organon* with which it has to make its way, than has philosophy, which regards that method with a speculative interest and very much as being one among others. So it may be argued: but quite possibly what is involved in this point of view is a difference of emphasis as compared with Papanoutsos's thinking on the general subject, rather than a radical disagreement. To the final stage in that thinking we may now turn.

The point, then, has been made first about history and secondly about philosophy that there is an important homogeneity between their aims and methods and those of the natural sciences. In the case of philosophy, however, Papanoutsos takes the comparison further by arguing that there is also a *continuity* between it and theoretical science; that theoretical science naturally leads into philosophy and is completed by philosophy. The argument is bound up with a distinction between two senses of "philosophy," a more general and a more specific, which Papanoutsos proceeds to outline. It is the more general with which we are concerned in the first instance when we think of the continuity that he wishes to stress.

The subject matter of science, he points out, can be classified (though not completely rigidly) into "nature," inorganic and organic, on the one hand, and "culture," relatively individualistic and relatively collective, on the other. This broad division between natural and cultural science coheres with a corresponding broad division between natural and cultural philosophy. There can be a matching *philosophical* way of looking at these matters— the inorganic world and organic nature, on the one hand, and consciousness and action, whether individual or collective, on the other. And there is a definite progression, Papanoutsos declares, from the subject matter and perspective of science to the subject matter and perspective of philosophy. [10] But of what kind? This is where Papanoutsos's reasoning becomes somewhat enigmatic, and requires a certain amount of reading between the lines.

The way in which philosophy "matches" science in the respects mentioned, it would appear, is not by acting as a mere theoretical acolyte; dutifully supplying a philosophy of nature, for example, which will simply be the principles of the corresponding science formalized and extrapolated to the limit—with science alone in a position to determine of what sort these shall be. The relationship between the sciences and their corresponding philosophies is more restless, more dynamic, than that. Philosophy for its part can and must raise such perplexities[11] as it sees in the conceptual schemes which it is either taking for study or constructing, partly or wholly on its own initiative, as thought experiments. It is for the benefit of science that it should do so. Whereas the methodology of science has much with which to stimulate philosophy, philosophical reflection about science has much to contribute to a scientific self-awareness, to the sensitivity of science as to what it has done and what it might do. From this point of view the so-called philosophy of science could be thought of as the conscience of science—more generally as science most deeply conscious of itself.

It is in this way, according to the author's reading of him, that Papanoutsos sees philosophy in its more general aspect. What he has in mind is that philosophical dimension of thought into which we may be drawn by thoughtful reflection upon our encounters with the world of nature or the world of human culture. But more than this: philosophy in its more general aspect is not just a dimension of thought entered upon from time to time and in response to specific, occasional "scientific" challenges. It is rather a habit of mind which, once cultivated, can (and ideally should) become *integrated* with the scientific; so that philosophy, as it were, takes possession again of its old inheritance. This is "philosophy" in a very old-fashioned but nonetheless respectable sense of the term, meaning human wisdom or knowledge, systematized in the more or less disciplined ways that we may call scientific, and as such completed and consummated theoretically by self-critical "logical" reflection.

Yet there is something unsatisfactory about terming philosophy so understood "philosophy in its general aspect." Philosophy so understood appears not to cover various activities properly called "philosophical," whose general features are simply different from those just described. Must philosophy as such be science-based, as seems to be the suggestion? Is not some philosophical reflection self-generating, in that its problems are those presented by the texture and the intractability of thinking as such? And is philosophy not preoccupied conspicuously by what lies outside the sciences, notably aesthetic, moral, and religious experience?

Those questions really answer themselves. Philosophy *is* autonomous in the ways and to the extent which they suggest. And there is not the slightest independent reason for supposing that Papanoutsos would not agree with this statement. The trouble lies in the terms "general" and "special," which he uses in the present context in order to make a broad distinction within the concerns of philosophy as a whole, as he sees them. What does "philosophy in its more special aspect" cover? Taken in this sense, philosophy concentrates on the most distinctive of man's "spiritual" functionings, the cognitive, the moral, and the aesthetic. It consists primarily, in other words, of the gnosiology, ethics, and aesthetics which make up the substance of Papanoutsos's own philosophical work. But does all this come within the scope of the "general" philosophy which has been described, i.e., as one of *its* more special applications? "Special" philosophy is so consistently of a "higher order" that it would seem not at all clearly to be a specialized development (or "specification" in a literal sense of the term) of "general" philosophy.

Perhaps, however, it is wrong to expect it to be so. Perhaps "special" philosophy as here understood is an offshoot of, rather than a specific manifestation of, philosophy in the "general" acceptation of the term. Such, it might be expected, would be the gist of Papanoutsos's answer to the difficulties just raised; and it appears to be the kind of answer which he actually gives, in one concentrated passage:

Here, too [sc. in "special" philosophy], we encounter the same fundamental feature of philosophical thinking [sc. as in "general" philosophy]: the advance "to the limit"—in depth, to the most basic of perplexities; in breadth, to the ultimate boundaries of knowledge. Now, however, science itself, as a pursuit, an exercise and a discipline, becomes a problem for investigation; and not alone, but in company with the practice of morality and with art, these three constituting the principal functions of the human spirit (some would add a fourth, namely the religious, with its specific dedication to the holy). In this light, philosophy more narrowly regarded transcends and consummates philosophy more generally regarded, which itself transcends and consummates science. [12]

The notion of transcendence, as it appears in the last sentence of this passage, is crucial. It serves to suggest that "special" philosophy is not just a permutation and combination, for special purposes, of concepts and principles contained in "general" philosophy. "Special" philosophy brings new resources, of its own, into play, and is in this way creative. Note also that it "consummates" philosophy more generally regarded. Just as general philosophy, ideally, integrates and takes possession of the scientific outlook, so special philosophy, ideally, integrates and takes possession of the general philosophical outlook. For reasons already mentioned, one should add that it also "completes" that outlook; but for present purposes the main point that has to be understood is that "special" philosophy, in a curious way, is more general than the "general."

Religion

Papanoutsos's final main theme in *Gnosiology* is the relationship of faith and knowledge. About it he speaks trenchantly and definitively. He recognizes that there can be a phenomenology of faith, not that there can be a gnosiology. Faith is faith and knowledge is knowledge. It has been a temptation for many philosophers but nevertheless a philosophical confusion to try to intertwine the two. The use of expressions such as "religious consciousness" and, more especially, "truths of faith" is liable to involve us in such confusion.

> We *can* speak, allowing ourselves a certain freedom . . . in our use of the term, of religious "consciousness," as we can of moral and artistic "consciousness." The sense, however, is not that which we give to theoretical "consciousness." . . . "Religious consciousness" signifies no sort of reference of religious claims to a general, objective scale of assessment by means of which their authority can be put to the test, but what is pervasive in and typical of . . . religious experience . . . as a peculiar mode of feeling, willing and thinking.[13]

What it comes down to, these remarks suggest, is that there can be no verification—or, it is important to add, falsification—of religious claims. In regard to the concept of "truth" there is a most striking contrast between Papanoutsos's position and that of Kierkegaard, who exploited the notion of *truth* in a way Papanoutsos would have to regard as a veritable paradigm of the confusion he complains about. Kierkegaard recognized what he termed "objective truth," the truth pursued in philosophy and the sciences, and at the same time repudiated it as being, from the point of view of the vitally religious man, trivial—a network of truths which can never, in the end of the day, capture for the individual the awful, paradoxical relationship in which alone he can see himself as standing before God. Such a relationship Kierkegaard described as "being in the truth," but "subjectively," not "objectively." By contrast, the whole of Papanoutsos's philosophy is written in a spirit of dedication to objective truth as to a supreme value—perhaps not that of the vitally religious man as he appears in Kierkegaard's powerful but idiosyncratic presentation, but that of man as an intellectually striving, enquiring, and theorizing being; to put it no more strongly, in at least one of his other great capacities. Papanoutsos would have little empathy with Kierkegaard in his attempt to convey the exclusive interest of "being in the truth" subjectively, so that religious "truth" is put upon a pinnacle, and scientific and philosophical truth fall away. However Kierkegaard's subjective stance should

be described, it should not be in terms of "truth": for Papanoutsos, part of the very concept of truth is that it should be objective.

The distinction of truth and error is applicable only in the gnosiological
context of *theory*. . . . Religious faith is another dimension of our
spiritual life; we cannot properly apply to it the gnosiological distinction
between the true and the false. [14]

So, while Papanoutsos describes various forms of religious experience with historical sensitivity and a sympathetic understanding of what they can mean to the individual, he himself maintains
a philosophical distance from them. He does so in spite of his
recognition that among the theoretical sciences may be included
theology. His position in this regard is that theology is "about"
religion and not "of " religion. [15] Theology may explain, order,
and systematize features of religious doctrine, but the point of
theology is not to induce faith. Faith, it would seem, comes
about otherwise; theology makes no converts. Of this very un-
compromising point of view it need only be remarked here that
Papanoutsos appears to be treating theology as being in a certain
respect analogous to logic and mathematics. Just as logic and
mathematics provide us with "modes of relating" which, arguably
at any rate, are not directly "about reality," so theology provides
us with "modes of relating" which are not directly part of the
content of faith. No new special access is involved in them.

Chapter Seven
Conclusion

At various points in this book reference has been made to Papanoutsos's humanism. The term has been meant to signify his absorbed interest in the nature of human achievement and human potentialities in the arts, sciences, and morality as displayed in the histories and more particularly as illuminated by the philosophies of these. But "humanism" in current usage tends to convey a certain antireligious tone, even a polemical spirit, which is conspicuously absent from Papanoutsos's work. He does not argue *against* religious values, religious ethical precepts, religious metaphysical claims, or any other tenets of religion—whether stridently like Nietzsche or in the more urbane tones of a David Hume. So long as these items are not "taken" in such a way as to intrude upon and obscure man's carefully controlled and disciplined efforts to think and create for himself, Papanoutsos has no animus against them. As an author he is simply not concerned, for example, with promoting the point of view that religious-mindedness is a delusion, or with propagating a "humanism" represented by the principle that there is nothing, no being such as to transcend man himself. On the contrary, his "humanism" is wholly positive. His review of "the world of the spirit"—to use his own description of the scope of his philosophy—finds in human art, thinking, and morality, regarded steadfastly as man's *own* achievements, abundant and indefinite interest and delight. If there is more to the story of human achievements than this (generously) limited point of view suggests, that is another matter. Papanoutsos is not prepared to declare that there is or that there is not. He has enough, and more than enough, with which to concern himself in what man "has it in himself " (so far as can be seen) to do and to be.

If Papanoutsos's whole record, not only as an author but also as an educational administrator and reformer, were taken into account, then the word "humanitarian" could aptly be applied to him. This book, however, has concentrated on his philosophical outlook and attitudes, for which "humanistic" is the better term. If the word "philanthropic" were to be understood in as literal a sense as possible, then Papanoutsos's thinking could be described as an interesting and outstanding example of philanthropic philosophy. He himself is not unacquainted with or insensitive to the darker side of human life, and to the capacity which people have for evil of varying degrees as well as for good. But from Papanoutsos's writing about art, science, morality, and so on, it is *respect* for persons that emerges; his analysis of human culture, balanced and critical as it is, could appropriately have as its epilogue a secular doxology.

Throughout this humanistic philosophy of his the key concepts, it may reasonably be suggested, are "freedom" and "creativity." These are indicative of Papanoutsos's concern with and vision of man as originator, rather than as an agent who functions, to however brilliant effect, in terms of abstract, general, and impersonal "laws" which, as it were, preempt all his ways of working; or even with man as a vehicle of inspiration, should the inspiration be thought of as anything but the illumination which comes more or less rarely as the reward of his own conscious striving to know, to express himself artistically, or to come to terms morally with his fellows. "Men swear by a greater than themselves," says the writer of the Letter to the Hebrews.[1] Papanoutsos's attitude is, in effect: let us see how far we can think of men as taking themselves without such a call for authentication. But the freedom and creativity which he sees human beings as capable of exercising in so many possible contexts do not in his view render the human scene one of anarchic arbitrariness. No one is more conscious than Papanoutsos of the need to educate people in cultural history, train them in scholarship and reasoning, school them in the arts, and accustom them to moral self-discipline, in order that freedom and creativity should be exercised not in a void but with point and purpose, on this side of what is communicable.

Papanoutsos is a philosophical polymath, in the best sense of the term, and his philosophical writings are massive. Their didactic sweep is far greater than this book, which has confined itself to some of the more personal parts of his philosophizing, will have conveyed. From first to last his work expresses a total earnestness about philosophy, a recognition of its crucial importance as a dimension of thought, and a belief in its virtues as a medium of general education. In holding fast to this belief Papanoutsos is in a great Greek tradition. Socrates, Plato, and Aristotle established it in the ancient world, but it has survived that world and come to life again from time to time, as during the long period of Turkish occupation when philosophy was looked to as the very matrix of Greek educational thought, its medium both of preservation and of revival.[2] Papanoutsos's philosophical writings exemplify the tradition outstandingly, in our own times. They may be claimed to do so more self-consciously and more expansively than those of any other twentieth-century Greek author.

Notes and References

Chapter One

1. Noted by the author in 1964. A slightly altered version appears in *Struggles and Tribulations on behalf of Education* (Athens, 1965), pp. 262–63.
2. Probably stressed most heavily in his *Ethics*, but worked on repeatedly in his philosophical writing in general.
3. The necessity but nonsufficiency of this condition represents another leading idea of his *Ethics*.
4. E. P. Papanoutsos, *Ethics* (Athens, 1956), pp. 12–13.

Chapter Two

1. This section is based principally on *Philosophical Problems* (Athens, 1964), pp. 11–28.
2. Ibid., p. 14.
3. Ibid., p. 21.
4. Ibid., p. 14.
5. Ibid., p. 16.
6. Ibid., p. 18.
7. This sub-section is based principally on *Philosophy and Education* (Athens, 1977), pp. 317–23.
8. Ibid., p. 320.
9. Ibid., p. 321.
10. Ibid., pp. 322–23.
11. Papanoutsos, *Philosophical Problems*, pp. 166–78 (on which this subsection is mainly based).
12. Ibid., p. 168.
13. Ibid., p. 169.
14. Ibid., p. 171.
15. Ibid., p. 176.
16. This subsection is based principally on *Reason and Man* (Athens, 1971), pp. 208–17.
17. Ibid., p. 213.
18. Ibid., pp. 213–14.
19. Ibid., p. 214.

Chapter Three

1. This subsection is based on *Gnosiology* (Athens, 1973), pp. 78–79.
2. Ibid.
3. Ibid., p. 79.
4. Ibid., p. 81.
5. Ibid., p. 86.
6. Ibid.
7. Ibid.
8. Ibid., p. 88.
9. Ibid., p. 91.
10. Ibid., p. 92.
11. Ibid., pp. 93–94.
12. This subsection is based mainly on *Gnosiology*, pp. 105–6.
13. Ibid., p. 105.
14. Ibid.
15. Ibid.
16. Ibid., p. 106.
17. See Chapter 2.
18. This subsection is based on *Gnosiology*, pp. 133–39.
19. Ibid., p. 136.
20. Ibid.
21. Ibid., p. 133.
22. Ibid., p. 134.
23. Ibid.
24. Ibid., p. 135.
25. James Adam, *The Republic of Plato* (Cambridge: Cambridge University Press, 1902), 2:510 (s.v. "Knowledge").
26. Ibid., 1:341 (478c).
27. The suggestion conveyed by an authoritative modern work on Plato's vocabulary is that in Plato ἐπιστήμη is, on the whole, a more comprehensive term than γνῶσις and that γνῶσις comes within the scope of ἐπιστήμη. See John Lyons, *Structural Semantics* (Oxford: Blackwell, 1963), pp. 176ff.
28. *Dizionario Sandron della Lingua Italiana* (Firenze: Remo Sandron, 1976); s.v. *epistemologia* (tr. by author).
29. Ibid., s.v. *gnoseologia* (tr. by author).
30. See, e.g., D. W. Hamlyn's definition in his article "Epistemology, History of," in *The Encyclopedia of Philosophy* (New York: Macmillan, 1967), vol. 3.

31. This subsection is based mainly on *Gnosiology*, pp. 195–202.

32. Immanuel Kant, *Critique of Pure Reason* (London: Macmillan, 1970), A51=B75 (Kemp Smith translation).

33. Papanoutsos, *Gnosiology*, p. 166.

34. Ibid., p. 199.

35. Ibid., p. 198.

36. Ibid., p. 201.

37. See Chapter 2.

38. Papanoutsos, *Gnosiology*, p. 195.

39. Ibid.

40. This subsection is based on *Gnosiology*, pp. 202–5.

41. Ibid., p. 202.

42. The term is introduced ibid., p. 203.

43. See, e.g., ibid., pp. 203–4.

44. Ibid., p. 203.

45. This subsection is based on *Gnosiology*, pp. 205–11.

46. Ibid., pp. 205 ff.

47. Ibid., p. 208.

48. Ibid., p. 211.

49. Ibid.

50. Ibid., p. 206.

51. Any such discussion would have to take into account the relatively extended signification, as against that of "science," of the Greek word ἐπιστήμη (employed in this context).

52. Papanoutsos, *Gnosiology*, p. 207.

53. Ibid.

54. In an essay entitled "The Perceptual Spectrum," in *Reason and Man*, pp. 26–36.

55. This is a close paraphrase of a passage on p. 29.

56. Papanoutsos, *Reason and Man*, p. 29.

57. Ibid., p. 35.

58. First published in English, in translation by the present author with the title "Concepts in Transformation," *Philosophical Quarterly* 12 (1962):3–10. ("Under" now seems preferable to "in" as a rendering of the ὑπό in the title.) Published in Greek in *Philosophical Problems*, pp. 147–154. In the following references the English page numbers are given in square brackets after the Greek.

59. Papanoutsos, *Philosophical Problems*, p. 147 [3].

60. Ibid., p. 149 [4].

61. Ibid., p. 153 [8].

62. Ibid. [9].

63. Ibid., pp. 153–54 [9].

64. Ibid., p. 154 [9–10].

65. Papanoutsos, *Gnosiology,* pp. 212–17.

66. Ibid., p. 212.

67. Ibid., p. 213.

68. Ibid., p. 214.

69. See the previous subsection entitled "Gradations of Knowledge."

70. Papanoutsos, *Gnosoiology,* p. 213.

71. Ibid., p. 214.

72. Ibid.

73. Ibid.

74. This subsection is based mainly on *Gnosiology,* pp. 242–58.

75. Papanoutsos uses this term here, and often elsewhere, unmodified and as a term of convenience, when (in the context of his dialectical method) it really should appear in quotation marks.

76. Papanoutsos, *Gnosiology,* p. 249.

77. The phrase is used on p. 241. The reappearance of "gnosiological" as a key term in this "epistemological" section may be disconcerting, especially as the point involved is simple: what a backwoodsman knows about some substance has its uses, but by and large what a chemist knows is both more interesting and more exploitable.

78. This is how Papanoutsos himself puts it on p. 251.

79. Papanoutsos, *Gnosiology,* p. 254. Papanoutsos illustrates this requirement by reference to some more-or-less dramatic changes in the historical progress of science, but cautions us against overemphasizing its negativity. Of course the pursuit of greater objectivity brings about sudden reversals of view. And it is liable to turn up "accidental" discoveries which may be revolutionary. But it *may* also provide the experienced observer with significant "nods and hints" (257).

80. Ibid., p. 278. It is not at all clear why "intellectualists" should deny "the formative impulse" of the human spirit, at any rate in all interesting senses of that phrase. See, in this connection, the second paragraph of the next subsection.

81. This section is based on *Gnosiology,* pp. 293–319.

82. "Geometry and Experience" (1921), tr. Jeffrey and Perrett, in A. Einstein, *Sidelights on Relativity* (London: Methuen, 1922), p. 28.

83. This term (in Greek, γόνιμος—sometimes translatable as "fertile") is an acknowledged borrowing from Léon Brunschvicg.

84. Papanoutsos, *Gnosiology,* p. 293.

85. Ibid., p. 302.
86. Ibid., p. 303.
87. Ibid., p. 311.
88. Ibid., p. 298.
89. Ibid. (the "simply" is Papanoutsos's own word).
90. Ibid.
91. Ibid., p. 315.
92. Ibid., p. 298.

Chapter Four

1. Papanoutsos, *Philosophical Problems*, pp. 141–44 ("Moral Theory and Moral Life").
2. Ibid., p. 141.
3. Ibid.
4. Ibid., p. 142.
5. Papanoutsos, *Gnosiology*, p. 418.
6. This study is partly historical, partly analytical. The greater portion of the analytical section was published, in English translation by the present author, in *Philosophy* (1959), 34:193–203, under the title "Freedom and Causality."
7. Papanoutsos, *Philosophy and Education*, p. 62.
8. Ibid.
9. Ibid., p. 66 (*Philosophy* 34:195).
10. Ibid., p. 67 (*Philosophy* 34:196).
11. Ibid., p. 65 (*Philosophy* 34:194).
12. Ibid., p. 74 (*Philosophy* 34:202–3). This passage, translated from a manuscript, reproduces the *Philosophy* version, which is slightly more compact than, although not differing in any essentials from, the published Greek one.
13. Ibid., p. 72 (*Philosophy* 34:201).
14. This section is based mainly on Papanoutsos, *Ethics*, pp. 367–86.
15. Ibid., p. 370.
16. Ibid.
17. Ibid., p. 377.
18. Ibid., p. 416.
19. Ibid., pp. 437–38.
20. The essay appears in *Reason and Man*, pp. 280–87.
21. Ibid., p. 285.
22. Ibid.

23. Ibid.
24. Ibid., p. 286.
25. Ibid., p. 287.
26. Papanoutsos, *Ethics,* p. 61.
27. Ibid., p. 117.
28. Ibid., p. 110.
29. David Hume, *A Treatise of Human Nature* (Oxford: Clarendon Press, 1928), Bk. II, Pt. III, Sect. III.

Chapter Five

1. E. P. Papanoutsos, "Five Definitions of Art in Quest of a Specific Difference," in *Philosophical Problems,* pp. 55–65.
2. Ibid., p. 62.
3. Ibid., p. 63.
4. With the author's acknowledgments to Bishop Butler and G. E. Moore.
5. Papanoutsos, *Philosophical Problems,* pp. 64–65.
6. Ibid., p. 49 (quoted from an earlier essay, "Aesthetic Experience"). Significantly, the "emotions" of everyday life are designated by the word συναισθήματα, and not, as are "aesthetic emotions," by συγκινήσεις.
7. Ibid., p. 50.
8. Ibid., p. 65.
9. See *Aesthetics,* pp. 133–61.
10. Aristotle, *Nichomachean Ethics* (London: Oxford University Press, 1931), 1109a (tr. Ross).
11. Papanoutsos, *Aesthetics* (Athens, 1956). p. 138.
12. Ibid., p. 139.
13. "Realize" translates πραγματοποιεῖ (ibid., p. 148).
14. Ibid., p. 153.
15. Ibid., p. 108.
16. Ibid., p. 155.
17. Ibid.
18. Ibid., p. 160. He notes on p. 158 that even arts as "abstract" as music and architecture are subject to certain temporal and spatial constraints, respectively, and to various limiting psychological factors: these constitute a form of "reality" which is not to be trifled with by composer or architect.
19. Ibid., p. 14.
20. Ibid., p. 23.
21. Ibid., pp. 18–19.

22. Ibid., p. 230.

23. See his essay "Aesthetic Experience," in *Philosophical Problems*, esp. pp. 51–54.

24. Papanoutsos, *Aesthetics*, p. 131.

25. Ibid.

26. Ibid., p. 132.

27. Ibid., pp. 259–264: also *The Catharsis of the Passions in the Aristotelian Definition of Tragedy* (Athens [French and Greek], 1953).

28. Papanoutsos, *Aesthetics*, p. 261. The phrases "prepare" and "love of humanity" are quoted from *Poetics* 1456a38 and 1452b38, respectively.

29. καθαρμός, which he prefers to κάθαρσις in this context.

30. Papanoutsos, *Aesthetics*, p. 259.

31. Ibid., p. 255.

32. Ibid., p. 258.

33. Ibid., p. 294.

34. Ibid., p. 295.

35. Ibid., p. 49.

36. Ibid., p. 249.

37. Ibid., p. 250.

38. Ibid., p. 129.

39. Ibid., p. 141.

40. Ibid.

41. Ibid., p. 156.

42. Ibid., p. 160.

43. Ibid., p. 398.

44. Ibid., p. 400.

45. Ibid., p. 318 and elsewhere.

46. Ibid., p. 319.

47. Ibid., p. 360.

48. Ibid., p. 361.

49. Ibid., p. 445.

50. Ibid.

51. Papanoutsos discusses this question in *Aesthetics*, pp. 401–13.

52. "Beauty" in this context translates ὀμορφιά (ibid., pp. 401–2).

53. Ibid., p. 52.

54. See, e.g., J. O. Urmson's paper "What Makes a Situation Aesthetic?" *Proceedings of the Aristotelian Society*, Suppl. Vol. 31 (1957).

55. Papanoutsos's term (*Aesthetics*, 406).

56. Ibid., pp. 406–7. The term "beauty" in the first line of this quoted passage now has to be employed to translate κάλλος. The significance of the difference will emerge in the sequel.

57. Ibid., p. 407.
58. Ibid. "Beauty" again translates ὀμορφιά.
59. Ibid.
60. Ibid.
61. Ibid., pp. 407–8.

Chapter Six

1. Papanoutsos, *Gnosiology,* Chapters 4, 5. The present section is based on pp. 320–74.
2. Ibid., pp. 330–31.
3. Ibid., p. 329.
4. Ibid.
5. Ibid., p. 369.
6. Ibid., p. 367.
7. Ibid., p. 264.
8. Ibid., pp. 375–76.
9. Ibid., pp. 380–87.
10. Ibid., pp. 380–82.
11. Ἀπορίες.
12. Papanoutsos, *Gnosiology,* p. 385.
13. Ibid., p. 394.
14. Ibid., p. 395.
15. Ibid.

Chapter Seven

1. Hebrews 6:17 (New English Bible translation).
2. See the author's *The Revival of Greek Thought 1620–1830* (Albany: State University of New York Press, 1970; Edinburgh: Scottish Academic Press, 1971), pp. 3–4.

Selected Bibliography

PRIMARY SOURCES

1. Major Works by E. P. Papanoutsos (arranged chronologically)

Das religiöse Erleben bei Platon [Religious Experience in Plato]. Tübingen: privately printed, 1926. Greek version: Τὸ Θρησκευτικὸ Βίωμα στὸν Πλάτωνα. Athens: Dodoni, 1971.

Αἰσθητική [Aesthetics]. Athens: Ikaros, 1948; 2d ed., 1953; 3d ed., 1956; 4th ed., 1969; 5th ed., 1976.

Ἠθική [Ethics]. Athens: Ikaros, 1949; 2d ed., 1956; 3d ed., 1970.

Παλαμᾶς-Καβάφης-Εικελιανός [Palamas-Kavafis-Sikelianos]. Athens: Skaziki, 1949; 2d (augmented) ed., Athens: Ikaros, 1955; 3d ed. 1971.

Ἐφήμερα [Passing Topics]. Athens: Ikaros, 1950.

Νεοελληνικὴ Φιλοσοφία Α΄ [Modern Greek Philosophy, Vol. 1]. Athens: Aetos, 1953; 2d (revised) ed., Athens: Zacharopoulos, 1959. Selection of Greek philosophical writings from seventeenth to early nineteenth centuries, with introduction.

La catharsis des passions d' après Aristote [Aristotle's Catharsis of the Passions]. Athens: L'Institut Français, 1953.

Γνωσιολογία [Gnosiology or Foundations of Knowledge]. Athens: Ikaros, 1954; 2d ed. 1962; 3d ed., 1973.

Νεοελληνικὴ Φιλοσοφία Β΄ [Modern Greek Philosophy, Vol. 2]. Athens: Zacharopoulos, 1956. Selection of Greek philosophical writings from mid-nineteenth to mid-twentieth centuries, with introduction.

Φιλοσοφία καὶ Παιδεία [Philosophy and Education]. Athens: Ikaros, 1958; 2d ed., 1977.

Ἐπίκαιρα καὶ Ἀνεπίκαιρα [Themes Topical and Otherwise]. Athens: Ikaros, 1962.

Ἡ Ἠθικὴ Συνείδηση καί τά Προβλήματά της [The Moral Consciousness and Its Problems]. Athens: Galaxias, 1962. 2d ed., 1970.

Φιλοσοφικὰ Προβλήματα [Philosophical Problems]. Athens: Ikaros, 1964. 2d ed., 1978.

Ἀγῶνες καὶ Ἀγωνίες γιὰ τὴν Παιδεία [Struggles and Tribulations on behalf of Education]. Athens: Ikaros, 1965.

Ἀμερικὴ [America]. Athens: Ikaros, 1966.

Λογικὴ [Logic]. Athens: Dodoni, 1970; 2d ed., 1974. Contains useful interlingual glossary of logical terms.

Ψυχολογία [Psychology]. Athens: Dodoni, 1970; 2d ed., 1972. Contains useful interlingual glossary of psychological terms.

Ὁ Λόγος καὶ ὁ Ἄνθρωπος [Reason and Man]. Athens: Ikaros, 1971.

Immanuel Kant. Δοκίμια [Immanuel Kant. Essays]. Athens: Dodoni, 1971. Introduction, translation, and notes.

Πρακτικὴ Φιλοσοφία [Practical Philosophy]. Athens: Dodoni, 1973; 2d ed., 1974.

David Hume. Δοκίμια. Φιλολογικά, Ἠθικά, Πολιτικά [David Hume. Essays: Literary, Moral, Political]. Athens: Kollaros [1974]. Introduction, translation, and notes.

Νόμος καὶ Ἀρετὴ [Law and Good Conduct]. Athens: Dodoni, 1974.

Τὸ δίκαιο τῆς Πυγμῆς [The Right of the Fist]. Athens: Dodoni, 1975.

Πολιτεία καὶ Δικαιοσύνη [State and Justice]. Athens: Kedros, 1976.

Ἡ Κρίση τοῦ Πολιτισμοῦ μας [The Crisis of our Civilization]. Athens: Filippoti, 1978; 2d ed., 1979.

Οἱ Δρόμοι τῆς Ζωῆς [The Paths of Life]. Athens: Filippoti, 1979.

David Hume, Δοκίμια Οἰκονομικά, Ἱστορικά, Πολιτικοκοινωνικά [David Hume. Essays: Economic, Historical, Sociopolitical]. Athens: Papazisi, 1979. Introduction, translation, and notes.

Τὰ Μέτρα τῆς Ἐποχῆς μας [The Measures of our Epoch]. Athens: Filippoti, 1981.

(In addition to the above, mention should be made of E. P. Papanoutsos's editing and direction of Παιδεία (later Παιδεία καὶ Ζωή [Education, later Education and Life]. Athens: Zacharopoulos, 1946–61, throughout its duration. This was a monthly periodical devoted to educational, literary, and philosophical themes.)

2. Work by E. P. Papanoutsos Available in English Translation (arranged chronologically)

"Freedom and Causality." Translated by G. P. Henderson. *Philosophy* 34 (July 1959):193–203. Reprinted in: *The Foundations of Knowledge* (see below), pp. 116–26.

"Poetry and Language." Translated and adapted by John P. Anton. *Charioteer*, no. 3 (New York, 1961), pp. 120–29.

"Concepts in Transformation." Translated by G. P. Henderson, *Philosophical Quarterly* 12 (October 1962):329–36. Reprinted in: *The Foundations of Knowledge* (see below), pp. 169–77.

"Moral Conflicts." Translated by John P. Anton. *Philosophy and Phenomenological Research* 24 (September 1963):73–82.

The Foundations of Knowledge. Translated by Basil Coukis and John P. Anton. Edited and with an introduction by John P. Anton. Albany: State University of New York Press, 1968. English version of Γνωσιολογία (see above).

"On the Moral Weight of Deontic Statements." Translated by E. P. Papanoutsos. In *Phenomenology and Natural Existence*. Albany: State University of New York Press, 1973, pp. 334–41.

"Law and Revolution." Translated and adapted by John P. Anton. *Philosophy and Phenomenological Research* 34 (December 1973):201–8.

"The Universe of Literary Creation." Translated by John P. Anton. *Journal of Aesthetics and Art Criticism* 34 (Spring 1976):301–3.

"The Aristotelian Katharsis." Translated by N. Georgopoulos. *British Journal of Aesthetics* 17 (Autumn 1977):361–64.

"The Gift of Art." Translated by N. Georgopoulos. *Journal of Aesthetic Education* 12 (October 1978):87–93.

SECONDARY SOURCES

Anton, John P. Review of Γνωσιολογία (1954). *Journal of Philosophy* 58 (December 1961):803–9. A well-balanced presentation, both sympathetic and critical, of Papanoutsos's approach to problems of knowledge.

Henderson, G. P. "Greek Philosophy from 1600 to 1860." *Philosophical Quarterly* 5 (April 1955):157–65. Critical study of Νεοελληνικὴ Φιλοσοφία Α' (1953). Comments on Papanoutsos's interesting introduction to the philosophy of an obscure period in Greek history.

―――. "Modern Greek Philosophy." *Philosophical Quarterly* 7 (April 1957):154–72. Critical study of Νεοελληνικὴ Φιλοσοφία Β' (1956). Comments on Papanoutsos's sure handling of the gradually "professionalized" Greek philosophy of the nineteenth and twentieth centuries.

Smith, Richard N. W. "Critical study: *The Fountain of Knowledge* (1968)." *Philosophical Quarterly* 20 (January 1970):67–76. A scholarly, perceptive, and authoritative evaluation of Papanoutsos's views on human knowledge.

Xydis, Theodoros. Το ἐκπαιδευτικό θέμα καὶ ὁ Ε. Π. Παπανοῦτσος [The Educational Question and E. P. Papanoutsos]. ΝΕΑ ΕΣΤΙΑ [Athens] 100 (Christmas 1972):232–42. Comprehensive and sympathetic assessment of Papanoutsos's contributions to education through teaching, authorship, and administration.

Index